EQUITY

EQUITY

How to Design Organizations
Where Everyone Thrives

Minal Bopaiah

Berrett–Koehler Publishers, Inc.

Berrett-Koehler Publishers, Inc.
1333 Broadway, Suite 1000
Oakland, CA 94612-1921
Tel: (510) 817-2277
Fax: (510) 817-2278
www.bkconnection.com

ORDERING INFORMATION

Quantity sales. Special discounts are available on quantity purchases by corporations, associations, and others. For details, contact the "Special Sales Department" at the Berrett-Koehler address above.

Individual sales. Berrett-Koehler publications are available through most bookstores. They can also be ordered directly from Berrett-Koehler: Tel: (800) 929-2929; Fax: (802) 864-7626; www.bkconnection.com.

Orders for college textbook / course adoption use. Please contact Berrett-Koehler: Tel: (800) 929-2929; Fax: (802) 864-7626.

Distributed to the U.S. trade and internationally by Penguin Random House Publisher Services.

Berrett-Koehler and the BK logo are registered trademarks of Berrett-Koehler Publishers, Inc.

Printed in the United States of America

Berrett-Koehler books are printed on long-lasting acid-free paper. When it is available, we choose paper that has been manufactured by environmentally responsible processes. These may include using trees grown in sustainable forests, incorporating recycled paper, minimizing chlorine in bleaching, or recycling the energy produced at the paper mill.

Library of Congress Cataloging-in-Publication Data

Names: Bopaiah, Minal, author.
Title: Equity : how to design organizations where everyone thrives / Minal
   Bopaiah.
Description: First edition. | Oakland, CA : Berrett-Koehler Publishers,
   Inc, 2021. | Includes bibliographical references and index. | Summary:
   "A fast and engaging read, Equity helps leaders create more inclusive
   organizations using human-centered design and behavior change
   principles"-- Provided by publisher.
Identifiers: LCCN 2021016171 | ISBN 9781523090259 (paperback) | ISBN
   9781523090266 (adobe pdf) | ISBN 9781523090273 (epub)
Subjects: LCSH: Diversity in the workplace. | Work environment. |
   Organizational sociology.
Classification: LCC HF5549.5.M5 B669 2021 | DDC 658.3008--dc23
LC record available at https://lccn.loc.gov/2021016171
First Edition

26 25 24 23 22 21   10 9 8 7 6 5 4 3 2

Book producer: PeopleSpeak
Text designer: Marin Bookworks
Cover designer: Sophie Greenbaum

For my brother.
My flaws are mine, and mine alone;
but all my goodness is because of you.

Contents

Illustrations

Figures

Photos

Foreword

Violent acts of systemic racism, sexism, heterosexism, and other forms of inequity are certainly not new in our country or in the world. And yet the recent killings of George Floyd, Breonna Taylor, Tony McDade, Nina Pop, and so many other Black people have led to far more awareness of inequities and a growing interest in addressing these injustices. It is almost prescient that Minal Bopaiah has written a book that addresses systemic inequity, and it should be read widely by individuals in diverse organizations who share an interest in, and hopefully have a commitment to, transforming their workplaces so that everyone can thrive.

This book is about very serious and complex attitudes and behaviors. Minal addresses how implicit bias influences how we design our systems, organizations, and even our culture; how we can use human-centered design to invite behavior change; and how to draw on principles of behavior change communications to effectively communicate inclusion, diversity, equity, and accessibility and thereby reduce resistance and sabotage in organizations. And she dares to compel leaders to make it their business to uphold democracy in service of creating a more equitable world. And yet this book is an easy read because Minal is a gifted writer and an engaging storyteller who draws on just the right amount of authoritative research, engaging examples, and personal experiences.

Minal clearly appreciates the power of brevity and of wit. This book, though slim in the number of its pages, is full of critical ideas, practical and doable steps for designing and creating meaningful change, and inspiring passages that have the possibility to incentivize anyone who reads them to create more equity and justice. And should we do so in ways small or grand, as this book promises, we will know the depths of our true humanity.

This is an ambitious promise, but I expect no less from Minal, who claims me as her mentor, a role I willingly and proudly play. As an African proverb says, "She who teaches must learn and she who learns must teach." A healthy, meaningful, and satisfying relationship always involves reciprocity. And so, over the years that Minal and I have known and worked with each other, we continue to learn from and teach each other about the similarities and differences in being cisgender Brown and Black women of very different ages, trained in different academic disciplines, but equally committed to social justice as we carry out our respective work to help organizations create more inclusive, diverse, equitable, and accessible workplaces.

In the interest of full disclosure, I must share that in addition to our mentor-mentee relationship, Minal and I have grown to refer to each other in familial terms—I am her Auntie J, and she is my Niecey. These forms of address reflect the reality that kinship is about more than lines of descent and marital relationships. Kinship is also about shared values, beliefs, and yes, shared hopes and dreams. Therefore, I cannot claim detachment in recommending her book. Rather, I claim lineage, for it is clear, despite our differences in both life and how we approach our work, we see the world through the same lens. And that world can be made beautiful through the virtue and practice of equity.

– Johnnetta Betsch Cole, PhD
    President and Board Chair, National Council of Negro Women
    President Emerita, Spelman and Bennett Colleges

The Virtue of Equity

On a bright August day in 1976, my Indian parents arrived in New York City with one suitcase, twenty dollars, and my mother pregnant with me. Without Google, they found their way from the airport to Greenpoint, Brooklyn, where they had secured medical residency positions at a local hospital. They began working at a time when New York City's financial mismanagement, high drug use, and racist "War on Crime" had created an atmosphere of civil war. My father saw more gunshot wounds in one night in the emergency room than in four years of surgical residency in England. For months, my very pregnant mother slept in a sleeping bag on the floor of their apartment. During the New York City blackout of 1977, my father and his colleagues triaged patients in the hospital parking lot illuminated only by the headlights of local fire engines. On an average day, security guards escorted them to and from the hospital buildings because so many medical residents had been mugged by people living with addiction who had been pushed to the fringes of society instead of invited into the hospital for treatment.

Eventually, my parents made it out of Brooklyn, moving to the greener suburbs of Staten Island, and started their own private practice—my mother in pediatrics and my father in colon and rectal surgery. (Their waiting room was always a prickly and entertaining cocktail of people young and old, most of whom didn't want to be there.) They bought a home and an office building, sent two kids to private school and college debt-free, provided for multiple family members, and contributed to their communities. *New York* magazine included my father in its annual "Best Doctors" issue eight times. In essence, they lived the proverbial American Dream, working their way up through hard work, determination, and honesty.

That, at least, is one version of their story. A fuller account of their immigration story starts much earlier, in 1965, when the civil rights movement successfully advocated for the Immigration and Naturalization Act, which grants US visas based on labor needs and family ties rather than country of origin. Before that, the US government had an immigration system that explicitly sought to "preserve the ideal of US homogeneity," meaning a White majority.[1] In other words, no amount of hard work, determination, or honesty would have been enough for my parents to thrive in this country if they had tried to enter before the 1965 act took effect.

But even that legislative act of inclusion had its own inequities. Starting in 1965, the US government began using its immigration system to take advantage of socialized education in other countries to fill its labor needs. My parents, both of whom came from rather humble backgrounds, earned medical degrees in India for a marginal cost (about fifty dollars per semester, according to family lore). That made them prime recruits for a country concerned with a shortage of physicians in the 1960s and '70s but wanting to avoid the expense of training doctors. While my parents came to this country with little monetary wealth, the debt-free medical education they gained in India was a distinct advantage. One might call it a **privilege**,* because this opportunity was certainly not available to the majority of Americans then—or now.

Seeing the System

When my parents and other Indian Americans are held up as members of a so-called **model minority**—characters in some sort of Horatio Alger tale in which the world is fair and everyone can succeed if they work hard enough—it reinforces a false narrative at best and is vicious **gaslighting** at worst. This is not to say my parents didn't work exceptionally hard; I witnessed many of the sacrifices they made to raise my brother and me, achieve their professional goals, and support their family and community. But if the US government offered socialized education as India and other countries do, I believe the percentage of American-born doctors with dark skin and poor parents would rival those in the Indian diaspora.

Instead, the United States has an education system tied to local property taxes. Most people don't question this approach to school funding; instead, they look to address disparities in educational opportunity and outcomes through redistricting and busing. But this is just rearranging the proverbial deck chairs on the *Titanic*. Outside of the United States, this funding design is rare. Most nations use general tax revenue to fund all schools equally and per capita, not by location.[2] As a German friend said of the US school system, "It just means the rich get richer and the poor get poorer." If we want to address the root cause of educational inequities, we need to have the courage to examine and reimagine how we fund our schools.

---

* Key terms are bolded throughout the text and defined in the glossary.

But with inequity built into our education system, we continue not only to produce inequitable outcomes but also to extract talent from other countries to fill gaps in our labor needs. Think about this: we are perfectly capable of meeting many of our labor needs if we simply invest in equitable education for all US residents, the way India and many other countries, including our European allies, do. But we *choose* not to.

This is not an anti-immigrant argument. Our culture benefits from immigration in many ways, and immigrants want to bring their talents to the United States for a host of reasons. (My parents, who eloped in England, have loved the idea of America since they were teenagers, not least of all because it offered them the freedom to be together. They were from different religions and different communities in India, and few people approved of them as a couple.) But it is a grave injustice—and a legacy of the "divide and conquer" mentality of **colonialism**—that the US educational system does not provide US residents with the quality of education to which immigrants have access in their countries of origin. Each group then blames the other for the country's problems (echoed in social media outrage like "Immigrants are stealing our jobs!" or "Americans are lazy and don't want to study or work hard!"). The US education system extracts human resources from other countries rather than investing in the talent and resources of its own residents to give them a fair shot at success.

This is systemic inequality, and the system was *designed* this way.

The first designer I heard talk about the intersection of systems and design was Antionette Carroll, founder and president of the Creative Reaction Lab, a nonprofit organization that helps design healthy and equitable communities. In an illuminating TED Talk, she says, "When I shifted my understanding of design from object-making to systems-building, I began to realize that systems such as discrimination, racism, sexism, and even poverty were designed by people that made intentional choices around exclusion."[3] Carroll's work—an inspiration for many designers, including yours truly—is centered around the fundamental truth that "systems of oppression, inequalities, and inequities are by design. Therefore, only intentional design can dismantle them."[4]

When we confront the fact that the Founding Fathers designed a system that benefited White men who owned property above all others, we begin to see the legacy of that design in our institutions, governance systems, and organizations. To be fair, designing for inequity isn't an American invention (although the United States did take it to another level, inspiring the Nazis to study US society so they could figure out how to codify violence and oppression for monetary gain and genocidal outcomes).[5] From European colonialism to India's Vedic caste system, designing for inequity appeals universally to those who are threatened—whether consciously or unconsciously—by the idea of sharing power with others.

Our country's saving grace—and the saving grace of many nations—is the values enshrined in the living documents governing our society. Values like **equality**, justice, life, liberty, the pursuit of happiness, freedom, and democracy have allowed generations upon generations of Americans—as well as people of other nations guided by their own intrinsic values of fairness—to iterate the design of their societies. When we dig into these values, we can redesign our educational and immigration systems—two systems that are interdependent—so that they produce equitable outcomes. That would mean that residents in the United States would have access to quality education regardless of their zip code and that immigrants would no longer be used as straw men in anti-Black rhetoric to justify oppression and disenfranchisement. We would begin to understand how systems, not just individual effort, lead to certain outcomes for individuals and groups.

With that understanding, just as we have designed for inequity, we can begin to design for **equity**.

Why Equity, Not Equality?

America's founding documents enshrine equality, so why I am focusing on equity?

First, let's unpack the difference between these terms. As a writer, I love words, but as the leader of a design firm, I admit that images sometimes convey complex concepts more powerfully. Figure 1, created by the Robert Wood Johnson Foundation, beautifully illustrates the difference between equality and equity.

Figure 1. Equality versus equity.
© 2017 by Robert Wood Johnson Foundation. Used with permission.[6]

Equality is when everyone has the same thing. Equity is when everyone has what they need to thrive and participate fully. Equity does not fault people for being different; it makes room for difference and then leverages it. In other words, equitable cultures, systems, and organizations are designed so everyone in the system has an equal chance to thrive. By *thrive*, I mean they have an equal chance to do work that fulfills them, live life authentically, and contribute their strengths to the community, organization, or culture of which they are a part.

This does not mean equality is bad. Sometimes equality is the appropriate response; in the movement for marriage equality, for example, "separate but equal" solutions like civil unions tip the scales in favor of injustice and second-class status for LGBTQ+ Americans. Only marriage *equality* could bring LGBTQ+ Americans the rights they deserve. But in other instances, equitable solutions, which allow for different approaches based on different needs, are sometimes ideal.

Equity has always been the middle child in the diversity, equity, and inclusion (**DEI**) space, the concept we all acknowledge is important but often hop over to address feelings of inclusion. And I get why: focusing on feelings is an easier and better way to promote DEI. Equity is more about strategy and systems, concepts that can make people's heads hurt. Personally, however, I care much more about equity than inclusion. Both are important, but the former drives the latter. Inclusion without equity is toothless; organizations end up talking about how to make people "feel more included" without doing the hard systems redesign that actually yields equal pay, more diverse leadership teams, and other signs of equal access to opportunity.

Originally from English law, the concept of equity was developed to "supplement, aid, or override common and statute law in order

KEY DEFINITIONS

For those who are unfamiliar with DEI, here is how I define inclusion, diversity, and equity. I am also passionate about incorporating accessibility into my work, which allows me to use the acronym **IDEA**.

Inclusion is a dynamic state where individuals and groups feel safe, respected, engaged, motivated, and valued for who they are and for their contributions to organizational and societal goals.[7]

Diversity refers to the differences—both visible and invisible—within a group or among groups of people. They can include differences in gender, gender identity, ethnicity, race, native or Indigenous origins, age, generation, sexual orientation, culture, religion, belief systems, marital status, parental status, socioeconomic status, appearance, language and accent, disability, mental health, education, geography, nationality, work style, work experience, job role and function, thinking style, and personality type. It's important to note that while a group can be diverse, an individual is not "diverse."

Equity, in its simplest terms, means fairness. In an equitable society, all people have full and unbiased access to livelihood, education, participation in the political and cultural community, and other societal benefits.

Accessibility refers to the design of environments, products, devices, and services so that people of various abilities can use them with ease. Accessibility refuses to fault individuals for the ways in which they are different and instead emphasizes the rights of individuals with differences to be full and participating members of society.

to protect rights and enforce duties fixed by substantive law."[8] In other words, it allowed societies to live the spirit of the law rather than the letter of the law. The legal concept of equity recognizes that people with power must use discretion when meting out legal decisions to ensure fairness.

Equity in the workplace is about designing a system, a culture, or an organization so that everyone has an equal shot, however they may define what they are shooting for (success, happiness, work-life balance, etc.). It's not about socialism versus capitalism or communalism versus independence. Rather, equity recognizes our interdependence and uses our collective power to create an environment where we all thrive and contribute our strengths. Moreover, equity gets us out of the hard work of constantly going against the system by creating a system that makes it easy to opt in to inclusive and equitable behaviors. Instead of looking for women to promote, for example, equity builds a system where women's needs are centered; thereby, having women in positions of leadership becomes logical and natural. (A more detailed discussion of gender equity follows in chapter 1.)

To be clear, I am not calling for the design of an idealistic utopia. To paraphrase a Buddhist expression, the world is strewn with rocks and thorns; trying to carpet it all is a fool's errand. I am intimately aware that life is inherently unfair; even if we were to solve all human-made injustices in the world, people would still die tragically and develop incurable diseases. By the end, life breaks everyone's heart.

However, amid such unfairness and heartbreak, I believe that the greatest expression of our humanity is the creation of fairness. In my mind, it rivals the creation of beauty and the expression of truth, which have been human pursuits since we were drawing on the inside of caves. Equity is how our human soul resists the temptation of revenge born of grief and sorrow. It is a virtue that leads us to a higher expression of our true nature. It's how we embrace interdependence so that we can design systems that work as well for others as they do for ourselves.

How Do We Design for Equity?

Moving toward the full expression of equity in an organization requires three preconditions:

1. Differences between individuals and groups are valued, not demonized or minimized.
2. People with power can see systems and how they influence opportunities for others.
3. People with power want to create more opportunity so everyone can thrive with their differences intact.

When these preconditions are present, designing a more equitable system, organization, or culture is possible. To understand these preconditions better, we'll start with an exploration of systemic bias in chapter 1, which will help readers see the larger system we're all working in and how implicit bias influences how we design our systems, organizations, and cultures. We'll also introduce a theory of change for designing a more equitable organization. Then in chapter 2, we'll discuss the approach used by Brevity & Wit, the company I founded, when working with clients on change initiatives. This approach incorporates human-centered design and behavior change management to allow for the creation of more sustainable solutions to IDEA challenges.

In chapter 3, we'll deep dive into the preconditions for equity as they relate to organizational leadership, exploring how storytelling can help leaders acknowledge their own privilege and power. This, in turn, allows them to become more effective advocates for equity by unmasking the invisible system for others. Once we have engaged leadership, we can then discuss how to create equitable outcomes and redesign a system to support those outcomes, as we do in chapter 4. A key part of this process is identifying observable behaviors and diagnosing obstacles that might get in the way.

In chapter 5, we'll discuss how to use the principles of behavior change communications to effectively communicate IDEA and reduce resistance and sabotage. And in chapter 6, we'll explore how to embed IDEA into marketing and communications and grow your ability to create a more equitable society. Since any organization with a social media account is now part of our media ecosystem, we'll pull from numerous examples in media that show the importance of screening content for **representation**, experience, accessibility, compensation, and harm reduction. In fact, throughout this book, you'll find examples that pull IDEA out of human resources and into the lifeblood of an organization, such as editorial coverage for news organizations and fundraising for nonprofits. Finally, the conclusion will discuss how to maximize your impact and create a more equitable world by making it your business to uphold democracy.

I admit this is an ambitious endeavor for such a slim book. Hopefully, brevity proves to be not merely a brand attribute but an asset in conveying some heady topics in a friendly manner (with some wit sprinkled in for good measure).

Before we begin, you are entitled to know a few things about me. I am bicultural, having been born in the United States to two Indian immigrants. When possible, I try to apply an intercultural lens to my writing. But given the specificity of design challenges and writing (the devil is always in the details) and the fact that I have never worked abroad for an extended period, I pull heavily from US organizations and culture. I am also a **cisgender**, heterosexual woman who waited until I was forty-one to get married. I'm child-free, and I have a graduate-level education in psychology and organization development. These experiences, and many others over my forty-three years on this small blue planet, have colored the lens through which I see the world. As an IDEA practitioner, I try to take a wider, more expansive view of the human experience than my life alone affords, and I am committed to doing the inner work required to address the shortcomings I may have developed from various types of privilege. But we are all a work in progress, so I write this with the humility that I always have something to learn.

Therefore, I'm interested in what you have to say about the ideas presented in this book. Please contact me at www.brevityandwit.com or www.TheEquityBook.com to share your thoughts, reactions, triumphs, and suggestions for improvement. Design is an iterative process, and I welcome your feedback.

Finally, some notes on language:

- I have chosen to capitalize all references to race and skin color, such as Black, White, and Brown. While race may be a social construct without scientific basis, applying capitalization equally to all categories ensures that this made-up construct is applied equally to all people's identities. Also, Johnnetta Betsch Cole, my mentor and the author of this book's foreword, taught me to do so many moons ago, and she is an elder in good standing whose counsel I do not question or ignore.

- Language is an evolving construct, particularly when it comes to identity. I have tried to omit offensive terms and aspired to choose those that are more inclusive. However, in the interest of appealing to an audience with a wide breadth of understanding of these topics, I have also tried to choose terms that do not interrupt the reading experience. For example, I have chosen to use LGBTQ+ instead of its more recent evolution to LGBTQIA+. I have also chosen to use the term Latine instead of Latino/Latina or the more recent iteration of Latinx. Latine uses Spanish-language norms to create a gender-neutral term, while Latinx has been criticized as an English-language adaptation that is foreign and unused by the Latine community.

- The field of diversity, equity, and inclusion is not without its own alphabet soup. DEI (i.e., diversity, equity, and inclusion) is the most ubiquitous acronym of the field today. But my background in clinical psychology makes me passionate about including accessibility, as people with physical and mental disabilities are often pushed to the margins even within the DEI community. The rearrangement of these concepts into IDEA (inclusion, diversity, equity, and accessibility) is not my invention but rather one I discovered through my collaboration with Inclusion NextWork, a global movement of millennial and Gen Z professionals committed to this work.[9] At the same time, I am neither offended nor put off when people refer to this field as diversity and inclusion, DEI, JEDI (J for justice), or any other permutation. As I explain in more depth in chapter 5, language is important, but it's not as important as doing the work. Horses before carts, friends.

Hopefully, transparency about my identity and choices will allow you to trust me more deeply during this expedition into equity. If so, I thank you. In a world full of noise, it's an honor to simply hold your attention for the duration of a book. I promise I won't take your trust or your attention for granted in the pages to come.

The Relationship between Bias, Systems, and Equity

My husband is a firefighter, which means he has no dearth of hilarious, poignant, and troubling stories about how resistance to diversity and inclusion manifests in workplaces, particularly among people who are not fond of change. One of my favorites is his story about three fire department captains who attended an out-of-state conference on diversity and inclusion. During one presentation, a speaker mentioned "LGBTQ."

"What does the Q stand for?" one of the captains asked.

"Queer," the speaker responded.

"Are you kidding me?" the captain responded. "Ten years ago, I literally got called onto the carpet by a supervisor for using that term."

I suspect—and sincerely hope—the speaker then explained the term's evolving use and its reclamation by LGBTQ+ advocates.

However, little of that sunk in. When the captain returned to his firehouse, his entire takeaway from the three-day conference was "Guys, we can say the word *queer* now."

This story always makes me laugh with both bemusement and despair. Bemusement because I sympathize with a captain for whom the world has changed too fast while he was literally putting out fires. At the same time, I despair for IDEA professionals. Is this really the top message we're delivering? Is this the takeaway from our efforts to host courageous conversations and spur people to "do the work"? And honestly, do we really need everyone to engage in a one-hour conversation about gender fluidity? *I'm* down for that, but I know my husband would rather do almost anything else, including all the housework he does on a regular basis while I write. And most troubling, are we implying in our conversations and reading lists that everyone needs a doctorate in social justice to be inclusive and equitable?

This is not a scalable solution. After hearing my husband's story, I realized we might all be better served if we simply told people like him and this captain, "Listen, when interacting with people directly in the field, always ask what pronouns they use." I wonder if that approach would yield more behavior change, since my husband's colleagues are often willing to follow the rules in the spirit of professionalism. And department policy has the added benefit of reinforcing inclusive behaviors through sheer peer pressure.

In short, instead of emphasizing personal growth and trying to motivate everyone to be better, we could design organizations in a way that it makes it *easy* to do the right thing. We could say, "Here are the rules by which your job performance will be judged." We could request specific behaviors that would ensure a more inclusive or equitable culture, such as asking new employees which religious or cultural holidays are most important to them and ensuring they have those days off. We could create organizations that are designed to work with the way the human brain works, which requires direction, motivation, and bandwidth to adopt new behaviors (more on this in chapter 2). We could be explicit in our expectations instead of asking everyone to be as passionate about IDEA as we are. This is how we can get scalable, equitable outcomes with less hand-wringing and frustration.

To achieve such equitable outcomes, we need the preconditions for equity. As we saw in the introduction, equity is possible when people with power

1. Value difference

2. See systems

3. Use their power to create more opportunity for others

In chapter 3, we'll discuss how leaders can value difference and see themselves in relation to the systems in which they live and work. Any individual is part of multiple systems: the organizational system of a company or nonprofit, the system or process by which work gets done, and the larger societal system, such as American culture and industry norms. We need to understand these larger societal systems because they're subtle and often made invisible by social conditioning. To help you see them, I offer a ten-thousand-foot view of the biases baked into the US societal system and culture.

Bias and Systems

Implicit bias—sometimes referred to as unconscious bias—is present in everything we do, including how we design systems. Bias happens when our minds automatically associate certain stimuli with certain thoughts, feelings, and behaviors. For example, when most of us see a red light, we automatically press the brakes without consciously thinking our way through interpreting the stimulus and responding to it. In many cases, as with this one, bias is a positive time-saver. Bias is detrimental, however, when our associations are based on stereotypes or bad data. If you don't know any transgender individuals (and 80 percent of Americans do not), you might assume certain traits based on media representations. Or if you have been taught to fear difference, you may be irrationally fearful when presented with any sort of difference, even if it poses no objective threat, as we have seen in the many incidents of police officers killing innocent children who are Black.

Understanding bias is important because it absolutely informs the design of systems. Mahzarin Banaji, a professor of psychology at Harvard University and a pioneer in the field of implicit bias, calls bias "the thumbprint of the culture on our brain."[1] *Culture* is just another word for how the system helps shape behavior among a group of people. The late Geert Hofstede, a renowned scholar who conducted seminal research on organizational culture at IBM and other organizations, describes culture as "the collective programming of the mind that distinguishes the members of one group or category of people from others."[2]

In today's America, most of us—regardless of our identity—have been collectively programmed to think of the "default" human being as White, male, straight, able-bodied, in early or mid-adulthood, Christian, and upper-middle class. Everybody else is "other." And so, most of our systems, processes, organizations, products, and laws have been designed for this "prototypical" individual.

Actor Anne Hathaway summed up this collective programming beautifully at a 2018 Human Rights Campaign awards dinner:

> The path to freedom, to equality, is currently being blocked by a big, heavy, almost invisible lie. The lie is not about whether we are equal. The lie is about whether our opportunities are. It's important to acknowledge that whatever my

actions have been, however hard I have worked, however the world may have marginalized me and my experiences, that my standing here, my ability to be visible to you, comes from the world unfairly rewarding my particular type of visibility. It is important to acknowledge that, with the exception of being a cisgender male, everything about how I was born has put me at the current center of a damaging and widely accepted myth. *That myth is that gayness orbits around straightness, transgender orbits around cisgender, and that all races orbit around Whiteness.*

This myth is wrong. But this myth is too real for too many. It is ancient, so it is trusted. It is a habit, so it's assumed to be the way things are. It's inherited, so it's thought immutable. Its consequences are dangerous because it prioritizes a certain type of love, a certain kind of body, a certain kind of skin color. And it does not value in the same way anything it deems to be other to itself. It is a myth that is with us from birth. And it is a myth that keeps money and power in the hands of the few instead of being invested in the lives of the free. (Emphasis added.)[3]

We have been collectively programmed to hold certain biases. Biases become racism, sexism, xenophobia, homophobia, transphobia, Islamophobia, ableism, and other isms and phobias when they are backed by power. When power backs bias, we get racist cops acting with impunity, like Derek Chauvin, who murdered George Floyd, and top executives, like Harvey Weinstein, sexually assaulting women for years and covering it up through nondisclosure agreements. We get Latine children in cages. We get transgender people being denied their right to health care.

An oft-repeated adage in the design industry is that great design should be experienced, not seen.[4] This makes racism a particularly well-designed phenomenon since, as designer, researcher, and educator Lauren Williams writes, "US constructs of race . . . have been so well designed that their existence is presumed to be fact and their operations and consequences are rendered invisible, insidious, ubiquitous, and relentlessly adaptive."[5] In other words, racism was designed to be invisible and to adapt. The same can be said of other systems of inequality and oppression. They are invisible thumbprints on our brain, influencing every decision, including our design of systems.

System Design

System design is the policies, laws, structures, institutions, traditions, and informal rules that govern how individuals operate within a given system. As I showed in the introduction, Americans—and many other people in different countries—are living in a system designed to work for some people over others, namely, White men with property. A number of iterative designs happened over hundreds of years to systematically advantage White, straight, able-bodied, Christian men with property (and property included enslaved people and women), including the following:

- The Indigenous people of America were racialized "subtractively." Laws were created mandating that the descendants of Indigenous people meet certain "blood quantum levels" to be considered American Indian. That is, they needed to prove they were one-half, one-eighth, or one-sixteenth American Indian to qualify as such. This ensured the eventual decimation of the Indigenous population. This benefited

White people because Article I of the US Constitution promises that the US government will provide Indigenous people of this land with social services in perpetuity; the eventual extinction of Indigenous people means that White people and other settler colonialists in this country could amass more of its wealth.

- Black people were racialized "expansively," meaning that "one drop of negro blood" qualified individuals for enslavement. This allowed White enslavers to multiply their free workforce through rape and enslave their own children.
- The Thirteenth Amendment ended slavery on the basis of race but continues to allow for slavery on the basis of criminality. The system of racism adapted again and began associating Black people with "criminals," leading to an exponential growth of incarcerated Black and Brown people in the last sixty years.[6]

We could go through the same historical exercise to look at the oppression of women, LGBTQ+ individuals, Jewish and Muslim people, and people with disabilities. This is how the system works for those it was not designed for: it is oppressive, it is discriminatory, and it continuously pushes back the starting line. It's no wonder some of us can't catch up. It's no wonder some of us are angry and tired. And frankly, it's no small act of nobility and grace that most marginalized people, to quote the activist Kimberly Latrice Jones, "are looking for equality and not revenge."[7]

The design iterations that perpetuate injustice and inequity rest on one central lie: **rugged individualism**, the idea that we can go it alone and that any and all success is due solely to our own effort. Unfortunately, this way of thinking is so implicit in our minds that it is hard to undo, and various innovations to create more equitable outcomes often perpetuate the biases of these systems of oppression.

One example is a financial app for high schoolers called Moneythink. Moneythink was created by a Chicago nonprofit to solve the problem of unaffordable college education by teaching low-income teens how to manage their money in preparation for college and employment.[8] But it doesn't address the soaring cost of higher education, the systemic causes of disparities in educational outcomes, or the racial wealth divide. (Black households hold less than seven cents to the dollar compared to White households, and White families living in poverty have about $18,000 in wealth, while Black families have none.[9]) Nor does it address disinvestment in public schools and in Black and Latine communities through gerrymandering, redlining (when lenders refuse to operate in certain neighborhoods for discriminatory reasons), predatory lending (when lenders use unfair tactics against borrowers), and other structures.

Instead, the app looks to individuals, not society, to solve the problem of unaffordable college tuition by "coaching" teens through the Free Application for Federal Student Aid (FAFSA) and teaching them to save (with no mention of the lack of high-paying jobs for high school graduates in their communities or employers' discriminatory hiring practices). In short, Moneythink blames victims for their own oppression and perpetuates the myth of "bootstrapping your way to success."

A less egregious example comes from my own life. Many years ago, my younger brother hit a rough patch, and I tried to get him on my health insurance. At the beginning of my career, I worked for an employer who offered a "self plus one" health insurance package. This was a gay-friendly policy that attempted to redress the absence of marriage equality laws at the time, but it was also being used by single parents and other individuals who needed to add one person, not an entire family, to their plans. Years later, I sought the same solution for my brother but found that most health insurance companies abandoned this policy after the legalization of marriage equality. To add my brother to my health insurance plan, I had to make him my "dependent"; that meant that he would be kicked off my plan if he earned more than $2,000 a month. And yet if I married a stranger of any gender, I could add them to my insurance plan without declaring them dependent or unfit to work. In fact, that person could go on to make more money than me and still be covered by my insurance.

The bias here is an American cultural definition of family that centers the "nuclear" family, a fairly recent concept in human history that negates the ancient appreciation for extended kinship networks. While the definition of family in this country has expanded to include same-sex couples, it still hinges on notions of sexual relationship and financial dependency. My brother is my first-degree blood relative, but many Americans may believe that I don't have a family because I don't have children. And so, the system centers a certain type of love, a certain type of relationship, above all others.

Designing Equitable Organizations in an Inequitable System

Designing an organization where everyone thrives takes ingenuity and courage, especially if you are trying to do so in a wider system that has bias baked in (US culture, for example). But creating an organization and organizational culture that fosters more equitable outcomes is possible, no matter your size or industry. Good designers know that we cannot allow the perfect to be the enemy of the good. Designers are inherently pragmatic, which is why design is such a powerful approach for creating more equitable organizations, so long as that practicality is coupled with an understanding of systems and the ability to discover the root causes of inequity, which we'll discuss more in chapter 2.

In working with clients to design equitable organizations, Brevity & Wit uses a sequential theory of change that starts with engaged leadership, defines equitable outcomes, and then redesigns the organizational system to support those outcomes (see figure 2). Engaged leadership, which we'll cover in chapter 3, requires seeing the system, as I hope you're starting to do, and retelling your story of success in a way that unmasks the system (both organizational and societal) for others. Defining equitable outcomes, as we'll discuss in chapter 4, is achieved by centering those who have historically been on the margins of the organization. It also requires identifying observable behaviors, such as making it policy that firefighters ask people for their pronouns when interacting with them. Then it requires identifying any obstacles to adopting that new behavior. The identification of those obstacles will allow you to redesign the system to support the new behavior. Throughout this process, as you can see in figure 2, we are also engaging in change communications that help generate buy-in and reduce resistance to IDEA, which we'll cover in depth in chapter 5. This theory of change will help create an organization whose impact can then be felt in the wider system and culture through media and marketing, as we'll show in chapter 6, or through its corporate and societal impact, as we'll discuss in the conclusion.

This model can work for both small and large organizations, although your impact may vary. Later in the book, I'll pull from examples of my work with Evans Consulting, a small firm of fewer

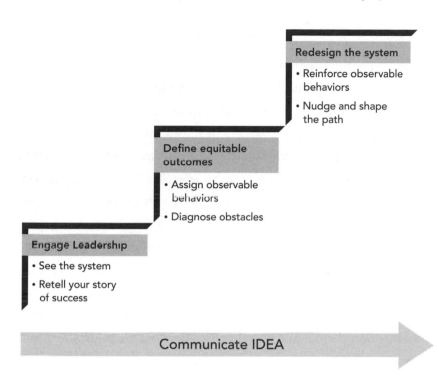

Figure 2. Theory of change for designing equitable organizations.

than one hundred employees, and with National Public Radio (NPR). Both organizations were able to establish equitable outcomes, but NPR understandably had more influence than Evans Consulting on the wider system of US culture because it is a larger organization with the ability to influence public consciousness. Evans Consulting does not have the power to change the entire industry of consulting and government contracting and, therefore, had to work within a smaller canvas of change. But what it was able to do did affect people's lives and the organizational system.

Centering and Rehumanizing

At the same time, when it comes to more equitable outcomes, changing who we center is absolutely critical, regardless of the size of an organization. We must design for human nature, but that also means designing for the *diversity* of human nature. Leaders must learn to *decenter* the identities Hathaway mentions and *center* those that have been pushed to the margins in the organization. And this, again, is why seeing the system and understanding systemic bias is crucial.

Centering people who need and deserve better outcomes means being aware of their historical and/or current exploitation and then examining how our current systems might be perpetuating that exploitation. Some may think that management books were developed during the Industrial Revolution; in fact, extensively data-driven labor manuals were written during the era of slavery to coldly calculate the worth and value of a human being.[10] The legacy of squeezing the most productivity out of a human body continues to influence the inequities we see in organizations today. As they explain in a 2020 *Harvard Business Review* article, researchers Robin Ely and Irene Padavic conducted an in-depth study of a consulting firm and found that the culture of overwork was more responsible than any other factor for the firm's lack of female leaders.[11] They found that women and men were *equally* distressed by the conflict between family and work. In fact, two-thirds of the male employees with children in the study expressed distress over this issue. Female employees with children, however, had been encouraged to make accommodations to address conflicts between work and family responsibilities, like going part-time or shifting to internal roles. Fathers, on the other hand, were generally expected to bury their feelings and work on, often to their physical and emotional detriment. "The real culprit was a general culture of overwork that hurt both men and women and locked gender inequality in place," Ely and Padavic concluded.[12] In other words, the culture of overwork was supporting old notions about gender norms as well as exploitative notions about employee productivity. In doing so, the culture was centering the needs of White men from centuries ago; it was not centering the needs of women or the needs of men in the twenty-first century.

This practice of centering people who need and deserve better outcomes is a deeply rehumanizing process. "Because so many time-worn systems of power have placed certain people outside the realm of what we see as human, much of our work now is more a matter of 'rehumanizing,'" esteemed researcher Brené Brown writes in *Braving the Wilderness*, her book on belonging in our communities, organizations, and culture.[13] We must begin to see the people who make up our organizations as people first and as employees second. We can no longer treat them as resources—even human resources—to leverage coldly and empirically, without warmth or care.

The need to recenter and rehumanize certain individuals and groups led me to believe in the power of human-centered design to address inequity. Of course, this isn't a zero-sum game. By centering those pushed to the margins, we often happen upon innovations that appeal to us all, such as text messaging, which was invented for people who are deaf and hard of hearing but is now enjoyed by everyone, or flextime, which was created to accommodate parents but has been a boon to workers seeking more autonomy over their daytime schedules. So, let's look at how we can leverage human-centered design to better serve the humans that compose our organizations.

A Design Approach to IDEA

2

If systems can be redesigned, then it makes sense to use a human-centered design (HCD) approach to achieving more equitable outcomes. At Brevity & Wit, we cross-pollinate HCD with behavior change principles to make this approach more effective for IDEA challenges. Doing so allows us to help clients from various industries expand IDEA beyond the realm of human resources. Also, by incorporating the principles of behavior change management, we apply what we know about human behavior and organizational development to solutions so that they can scale across an organization rather than languish as well-intended but ineffective efforts.

The Story of Embrace

Part of Brevity & Wit's approach to IDEA was born out of our partnership with Rajan Patel, coinventor of the Embrace infant warmer and cofounder of Dent Education, a nonprofit that teaches design thinking, making, and entrepreneurship to Baltimore high school students. In 2017, I attended a talk by Rajan, where he shared the story about cocreating Embrace with classmates from Stanford and various mothers, health-care workers, and families in India. It was there that I saw HCD's full power to create solutions that value difference.

Rajan's story begins when he was an undergrad at the Hasso Plattner Institute of Design at Stanford University (commonly referred to as Stanford's d.school), where he and fellow students turned a class project on creating a low-cost incubator for premature babies into a nonprofit organization they launched in India. The infant mortality rate in India is exceptionally high, and many premature babies lack access to incubators and other essential medical equipment. A solution seeking equality might provide all Indian hospitals with the kind of incubators used in the United States and Europe. Mission-driven organizations might rally around this solution, believing they can "scale good" using "market-based practices." And in fact, many people (mostly successful members of the Indian diaspora who wanted to support their hometowns or villages) have donated this expensive equipment to local facilities. Rajan was astonished to see it collecting dust in rural health-care facilities. He heard nurses say, "I have no idea how to use it and am afraid. I'd rather stick to what we know instead of putting an at-risk baby into something I might mess up and cause more damage with."

So Rajan and his classmates took a different approach—one that did not presume the superiority of Western medicine and sought first to understand the lived experiences and needs of patients and health-care workers in India. Through a human-centered design process (also referred to as "design thinking") that starts by empathizing with "end users," Rajan's team discovered that (1) many Indian mothers give birth in their homes, far from the nearest hospital; (2) with unreliable electricity, incubators are often useless in hospital settings; and (3) many mothers, even when in a hospital, dislike placing their babies in unfamiliar medical devices and grow depressed upon being separated from their newborns.

Rajan and his team put human needs and realities at the center of their design process and began designing a solution for *Indian* families and health workers. They interviewed mothers, nurses, doctors, hospital administrators, and mothers-in-law (who typically have a say in child-rearing choices in India). They created proto- types and tested them with interviewees. After years of work, they went to market with the Embrace infant warmer (photos 1 and 2), a swaddle unit that uses a "phase change pack" (also referred to as a "wax pack") to keep infants at an ideal 37°C. The phase change pack can be heated with a nonelectric heater or an electric heater; the latter was requested by hospital staff who wanted a device that could be heated by a generator, so long as it didn't need a constant supply of electricity. These options allow the swaddle unit to be

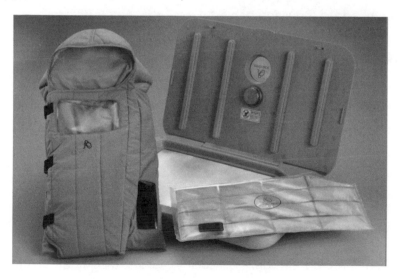

Photo 1. The Embrace infant warmer.
Photo courtesy of Embrace Innovations.

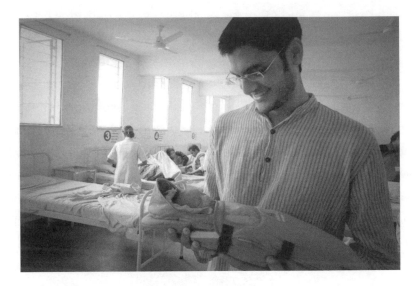

Photo 2. Rajan Patel holding a baby in the Embrace infant warmer.
Photo courtesy of Rajan Patel.

used in home or hospital settings; to date, it has saved more than three hundred thousand babies' lives.

This is what an equitable solution looks like: it is context specific, with no added burden on those whose needs have been ignored. It is not *equal* to the medical incubators used in the West, nor is it better or worse. It is different because the needs of Indian mothers and babies are different. This approach reflects one of the core preconditions of equity: embracing differences instead of demonizing or minimizing them.

Applying Human-Centered Design to IDEA

Human-centered design, particularly as it's taught at Stanford's d.school and practiced at IDEO, a global design firm, is often broken into five practices: empathize, define, ideate, prototype, and test.

However, HCD, as originally envisioned and practiced at Stanford and IDEO (two organizations that made it famous in innovation circles), has also gotten a bad rap at times, in part for a profound lack of diversity among designers. A survey conducted in 2019 by AIGA, a professional association for design, found that fully 71 percent of designers identify as White/Caucasian.[1] In an article entitled "Design Has an Empathy Problem: White Men Can't Design for Everyone," designer Jesse Weaver eloquently explains how "the design process they [IDEO] championed and popularized perpetuates a belief that any person can design for anyone else, and this belief plays a central role in design's continuing lack of diversity."[2]

This fallacy has led some well-intentioned professionals to design poor products that reinforce systemic inequality, such as the Moneythink app discussed in chapter 1, which was developed using HCD. Given this, it may seem odd for me to promote this practice. But as Rajan and I have discussed over the years, HCD has been both misunderstood and overused, and needs to be iterated upon. (If you are interested in exploring equity-centered design processes, I highly recommend checking out Antionette Carroll's Creative Reaction Lab and the Equity Design Collaborative.) Let's dive deeper into each phase of human-centered design and explore how we can use this process to advance IDEA in organizations.

Empathize

In 2010, I was the managing editor for a news site dedicated to covering the UN development goals. Many reporters would voice their frustration about how "no one cares" to do anything to help people experiencing famine, war, oppression, and poverty in other countries. "They won't give up their sneakers made in sweatshops or divest from index funds that back arms manufacturers," they lamented.

I noted a tone of intolerance in their voices. I would advise them, "Write your story for a single working mother of two kids, one of whom has a major illness. I guarantee you that she cares about the state of the world and wants to make it better. But she is pressed for time and money and can't afford to buy the sustainable sneakers that cost more than her paycheck or spend extra hours researching stocks. Buying from Walmart and investing in low-fee index funds allows her to spend more time with her kids and ensure they will be taken care of in the future. Find a way to advocate for sustainable solutions that work for her."

Both human-centered design and the work of IDEA place a high value on empathy. And yet shockingly few grasp what empathy actually is. In both the design world and social justice circles, change enthusiasts can fall into the trap of calling people out for being wrong instead of "calling them in" to be better, as academic and activist Loretta J. Ross recommends.[3] Intellectual snobbery is a serious detriment to advancing equity and should be fundamentally rejected by those seeking equitable solutions.

People also confuse empathy with connection. When leading workshops to help people craft communications around IDEA initiatives, I sometimes ask one person to role-play a person in the organization who is resistant to IDEA efforts. The other participants must then identify the target audience member's values. A CFO, for example, likely values financial stability and profitability. Participants will often try to convince the CFO to value IDEA for its own sake. They believe that if they stay connected—if they are polite and socially skillful—they are being empathic.

But connection is not empathy. Empathy is *understanding why* the CFO values financial stability and profitability and respecting them for it. That doesn't mean the CFO doesn't value IDEA at all. It simply means they have different priorities or different primary values. When designing for equity, the objective is not to get everyone to think the same, have the same values, or believe the same things. The objective is to design a world where differences are valued. That begins with embracing differences in personal values (so long as none rest on the **dehumanization** or oppression of others).

This level of understanding or empathy often comes more from a **perspective-gathering** approach than the perspective-taking approach originally promoted in HCD. Perspective-gathering asks people about their experiences instead of presuming anyone can place themselves in another person's shoes. Social science backs this approach. Behavioral scientist Nicholas Epley found through numerous experiments that perspective-*taking* is actually quite flawed. Understanding someone else's point of view comes not from imagining it but from asking and listening—from gathering someone's perspective rather than taking it. As Epley explains in an article in *Behavioral Scientist,*

> Trying honestly to put yourself in another person's shoes combines your intuitive tools of egocentrism and stereotyping in the hopes of maximizing the benefits of both. You take what you already know about others and then use your own brain to simulate the results if you were someone else. . . .
>
> . . . If you don't really know what it's like to be poor, in pain, suicidally depressed, at the bottom of your corporate ladder, on the receiving end of waterboarding, in the throes of solitary confinement, or to have your source of income soaked in oil, then the mental gymnastics of putting yourself in someone else's shoes isn't going to make you any more accurate. In fact, it might even decrease your accuracy. . . .

What's more problematic is that if your belief about the other side's perspective is mistaken, then carefully considering that person's perspective will only magnify the mistake's consequences. This is particularly likely in conflict, where members of opposing sides tend to have inaccurate views about each other.[4]

The limitations of perspective-taking are often most pronounced in matters regarding race, where many people have been led to believe that they are "color-blind." The problem is that, as DEI expert Heather Caruso notes, implicit bias research shows that "noticing race happens so quickly (less than one-seventh of a second) that we cannot consciously control it."[5] Equity requires the humility to admit we are all limited by the skin we inhabit, and we need empathy to take the time to ask and *believe* other people's different life experiences.

The power of perspective-gathering is evident in the repeal of "Don't Ask, Don't Tell," a Clinton-era policy that banned members of the LGBTQ+ community from serving openly in the military. When President Obama was considering repealing this policy, more than 1,000 retired military officers wrote an open letter (using a perspective-taking approach) expressing concern that repealing the ban would lower troop morale and erode unit cohesion. Meanwhile, Pentagon leaders asked more than 150,000 soldiers and military spouses about the issue. As Epley notes in his article, around 70 percent said that repealing the ban would have no effect. A nearly identical percent reported having worked with a gay service member. Of those, the vast majority (92 percent) said it didn't affect their ability to work together. Because of this perspective-gathering data, then–Defense Secretary Robert Gates pushed for the repeal, saying it "would not be the wrenching dramatic change that many have feared and predicted."[6] President Obama repealed the policy in 2010.

As Epley writes, "Others' minds will never be an open book. The secret to understanding each other better seems to come not through an increased ability to read body language or improved perspective taking but, rather, through the hard relational work of putting people in a position where they can tell you their minds openly and honestly."

Define (and Diagnose)

In HCD, the practice of defining problems usually results in a problem statement framed as "How might we . . .?" A product innovation team might complete the question by asking, "How might we design a product to keep premature babies alive in India?" An urban planning organization might ask, "How might we make public spaces more accessible for people with disabilities?"

In an organization, the question could point to more equitable outcomes: "How might we ensure that there are as many people of color in leadership positions as there are in the company as a whole?" or "How might we diversify our news sources to represent the demographics of the country?" or "How might we increase racial diversity on our board of directors?"

The bridge between more equitable outcomes and measurable results is observable behaviors. Observable behaviors give people with diverse backgrounds the rules of the road in an organization, the ability to understand those unspoken cultural norms that can contribute to one's success or failure. We'll spend more time in chapter 4 talking about the importance of observable behaviors and how to develop them.

Diagnosing obstacles to the behaviors you want to see in the organization is also important. This is a step Brevity & Wit added to the standard HCD model, based on our knowledge of behavior change management. The best framework I have found for diagnosing obstacles is in the book *Switch: How to Change Things When Change Is Hard*, written by real-life brothers and business consultants Chip and Dan Heath. *Switch* succinctly sums up decades of psychological and neuroscientific research on behavior change. In short, for behavior change to happen, two factors must be in place: sufficient motivation and sufficient direction. But because self-control is a limited resource, a third factor is critical—an easy path to reduce mental bandwidth.[7] Let's dive into each.

For change to happen, people must feel inspired or motivated or feel the pain of hanging on to an old behavior. Inspiring motivation for change is the primary technique in most IDEA workshops; the most effective workshops allow people to *experience* their biases, not merely rationalize why they exist. One powerful way to do this is through the Big Decision, an exercise developed by IDEA practitioners Howard Ross and Leslie Traub and featured in *The Inclusion Nudges Guidebook*.[8] In this exercise, workshop participants are broken into groups. Each group is asked to evaluate a potential job candidate. Participants read the materials and rate, both individually and as a group, how likely they would be to hire the candidate. Answers can range from 0 to 100 percent, and the spread is often wide within and between the groups. Participants then learn that all groups have been given the same résumé and bio, with only the name, photo, and some identifying details (like pronouns) changed. This often triggers an aha moment, as participants experience the psychological pinch of seeing their own biases in decision-making and begin to consider strategies for mitigating them.

Feelings, however, are rarely enough to establish long-term change; clear direction is also needed. When I worked with NPR to help it diversify its sources for news coverage, I found that most of the organization's news managers believed that a diversity of voices is imperative to maintain relevance. But news managers didn't know how to appropriately diversify their sources. What does the process look like? they wondered. How do we implement it without "tokenizing"? Do we wait to file a story so we can get more diverse sources? These are all reasonable questions, and part of my engagement involved addressing them by creating an achievable objective, which we will explore in chapter 4.

Sufficient motivation and direction make behavior change more likely, but it's no guarantee. That's because people's minds are already taxed by our complex world, especially in individualistic societies like the United States, where we are expected to do everything for ourselves. (As one writer wrote during the pandemic, "Other countries have social safety nets. The US has women."[9]) The solution, according to the Heath brothers, is to shape the path.[10] In other words, we must reduce the cognitive and emotional load of behavior change and make new behaviors easy to adopt.

Shaping the path might be as simple as creating meeting room signs that remind people to face a camera during virtual meetings so coworkers with hearing difficulties can read lips. Or it might mean devising a promotion process where everyone is automatically promoted after three years of positive performance reviews unless there's a clear reason not to do so.

For your convenience, I've provided the Define and Diagnose Cheat Sheet that Brevity & Wit uses when we are identifying obstacles to equity in an organization (figure 3). Each type of obstacle has a logical solution, which we'll discuss more in chapter 4.

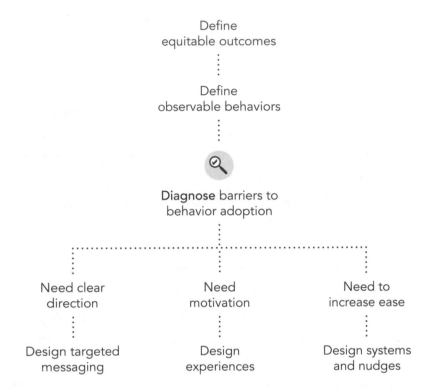

Figure 3. Brevity & Wit's Define and Diagnose Cheat Sheet.

Ideate

Ideate (or, in its noun form, *ideation*) is a fancy word for brainstorm. It's probably the practice most closely associated with HCD because of its power to unleash creativity in people and groups, especially in those who think they lack it. It also often involves the fun use of sticky notes.

The most basic and common ideation method is to ask participants to sketch solutions to the design challenge on sticky notes—one idea per note. The practice of sketching is not meant to induce competitive drawing skills. Many of us are visual learners, and images and sketches can convey concepts more quickly than words. However, if you are codesigning with people who are blind or visually impaired, amend this process. Use smartphone apps to articulate written words on sticky notes or ask other participants to read the content aloud.[11]

Be sure to establish guidelines for good brainstorming. Here are some sample ground rules from which you can add or subtract, based on the unique needs of your design group:

- Explore wild ideas.
- Ban judgment or naysaying during the brainstorm.
- Hold one conversation at a time so everyone can participate.
- Build off each other's ideas.
- Be visual.
- Go for quantity.
- Stay focused.

You can use the Define and Diagnose Cheat Sheet to know whether your intended audience needs more direction, more motivation, or an easier pathway to change during your brainstorm. If your audience needs clearer direction about an observable behavior, then you need to design more effective communications. If your audience needs more motivation to adopt an observable behavior, then you need to design an experience or set of experiences that allow people to feel the need for change. If your audience has direction and motivation but is short on time or mental bandwidth, then you need to design better systems and processes.

Don't worry about getting it perfect. The ideate phase should leave you with a plethora of ideas to prototype and iterate.

Prototype

As IDEO leaders and brothers Tom and David Kelley famously said, "If a picture is worth 1,000 words, a prototype is worth 1,000 meetings."[12]

Prototypes allow for feedback early in the development process through testing, which enables designers to course correct before investing too much time or effort. When designing equitable organizations, your prototype may involve the use of storyboards, draft messaging, website wireframes, brochures, outlines of experiences, process charts, drawings, or other tools and materials.

How does a group decide which idea to prototype? This process can be uncomfortable for those committed to inclusion, who may see excluding ideas as tantamount to excluding people. People with perfectionist tendencies may also have difficulty with this process if their ideas are rejected, especially if their self-worth comes from external acceptance. It takes skill to throw out bad ideas without making people feel bad about coming up with them, but it is essential to the design process.

The way to manage this tension is to create a clear and transparent decision matrix for evaluating ideas. Instead of asking, "Which idea do you like or feel passionate about?" build a decision matrix that asks the following questions (or make up your own):

- Which idea gets us closest to our desired outcome?
- Which idea is most likely to work for the people we are centering?
- Which idea can we afford financially?
- Which idea do we have time to test and implement?
- Which idea is the most inclusive?
- Which idea is the most equitable?

Real, sustainable change requires focus. Explain to your design cohort that focusing on one idea doesn't mean other ideas are invalid; it simply means that the design cohort can't commit the resources to acting on all of them now. As Steve Jobs, the late cofounder explained at Apple's 1997 Worldwide Developers Conference, "Focusing is about saying 'no.' You've got to say 'no, no, no' and when you say 'no,' you piss off people." Ten years later, he reiterated this belief when he said, "Focus means saying no to the hundred other good ideas. I'm actually as proud of the things we haven't done as the things I have done. Innovation is saying 'no' to 1,000 things. You have to pick carefully."[13]

Test

Feedback is a gift. Good designers live by that creed.

Testing is a continuation of perspective-gathering. Organizations seeking to design for equity should never be shy about asking employees and customers for their opinion. If you're designing for clear observable behaviors, testing is easier because observations become your metrics of success.

However, designers for equity must be mindful of managing for power dynamics. Feedback is best when people are candid, but power differentials often inhibit candor. If you don't have a high-trust environment or the ability to navigate conflict skillfully, don't expect high-quality feedback.

That's why being familiar with power and the qualities of inclusive power is helpful for designers and leaders.

Design and Power

Dacher Keltner, a social psychologist, defines power as the ability to make a difference in the world.[14] As we'll see throughout this book, design is enormously powerful in this regard. Designers can shape people's moods, behaviors, lives, and careers. We can make life easier or harder for people; thus, we have a responsibility to use this power wisely.

Sadly, however, power is used indiscriminately by some and unconsciously by others. People who value power *over* others use it negatively—to oppress, dominate, exclude, and extract. In her book *The Power Manual*, Cyndi Suarez, editor in chief of *Nonprofit Quarterly*, refers to the supremacist approach to power as "the taking of more than one's share."[15] It's not hard to see this use of power in colonialism and **predatory capitalism** and draw a line from these attitudes to our current climate crisis.

Meanwhile, people who use power unconsciously often aspire to be egalitarian but, in doing so, are uncomfortable about any discussion of power. They deny their power in an attempt to minimize its impact, just as some people deny differences. But denial—either of power or differences—does not yield more equitable or egalitarian outcomes. Instead, people inadvertently use their power to oppress—without awareness of the harm they are doing.

Designers must be aware of their power when they are designing. There's a certain naïveté among some design thinkers who believe they can apply the human-centered design process to any context. Rajan Patel first became aware of this shortcoming in the HCD process when working in India and grew more aware of it as cofounder and CEO of Dent Education.

Dent Education's summer internship program encourages teenagers to prototype their designs and seek feedback about them from strangers, just as professional design teams do. One team—comprising Black teenage boys—wanted to prototype a luxury doghouse. Knowing their market, they took the prototype to an upscale neighborhood and asked passersby for their thoughts. Some people stopped and talked, and some walked on. One White woman took the time to give detailed feedback while also visibly holding a bottle of pepper spray in her purse the entire time.

This implicit use of power—treating Black children as threats when they are trying to design helpful new products—is profoundly harmful. It might have been an unconscious act. Nevertheless, its impact is heartbreaking: those boys learned that in their most curious and helpful state of mind, some people see them as a threat. To avoid doing harm like this, we must all work to understand and take responsibility for how we use power and how we act on our implicit biases in various contexts.

When it comes to designing more equitable organizations, an understanding of power is vital. We should aspire to a liberatory approach to power, which, according to Suarez, views differences as strengths, entertains interdependence as an option, and relies on our ability to create what we want and need to thrive.[16] This sort of power is relational, working from a spirit of trust that all parties' needs can be met. In addition, when designing organizations, we need to identify and work with **power brokers**. As IDEA consultant and author Mary-Frances Winters says, "Allies are important but are not always in a position to influence systems. A power broker is typically an industry insider who is familiar with other important individuals and groups. By using these networks, they are able to exert influence and make decisions that influence systems."[17] Many initial attempts at IDEA within organizations backfire due to a lack of understanding of power and influence. Organizations are not democracies; CEOs cannot be voted out. Grassroots efforts are not as effective in organizations as they are in our larger society. As Dr. Cole taught me, we must start with leaders and others who have the power to design, redesign, and influence the system.

Observable behaviors can help ground discussions of power and how to use it in a liberatory manner. DEI consultant Julie

Diamond discusses seven behaviors of inclusive power in her Diamond Power Index:[18]

Empowerment: allowing others to contribute meaningfully by creating conditions for them to succeed. Includes mentoring, coaching, providing resources and information, clarifying tasks, roles, and deliverables, and taking an active interest in the development of others.

Conflict Competence: being able to engage productively despite differences, conflicts, and disagreements. Includes the ability to raise controversial topics, have difficult conversations, hold people accountable, deliver straightforward feedback, and intervene appropriately when interpersonal difficulties and conflicts arise.

Respect: being considerate of others, behaving on a principle of mutual respect without discrimination, hostility, or rudeness. Requires awareness of your communication style and how you come across to others—not only in your spoken words, but also in your nonverbal signals, tone of voice, and in both digital and face-to-face communication.

Fairness: treating others equitably regardless of your personal preferences, biases, or beliefs. Includes making sure that opportunities for development and advancement are distributed evenly, and being aware of how your biases intersect with the choices and decisions you make.

Approachability: inviting participation, making it safe to speak up and contribute, and being available and supportive. Approachability means being able to receive feedback, inviting others to speak up, easing pain points, modeling vulnerability, and creating an atmosphere that encourages creativity, risk-taking, and collaboration.

Discretion: keeping information confidential and refraining from gossip. Discretion means being professional in how, what, and with whom you share information. It includes keeping confidential information private, not venting, criticizing, airing grievances publicly, or discussing work matters, people, and the organization in an inappropriate context.

Judiciousness: placing the needs of the organization, the team, or the project ahead of your own self-interest. Being accountable to the role and using it to advance the needs of the greater good rather than your own agenda or personal needs.

These qualities of inclusive power are necessary for equitable leaders. As we'll see in the next chapter, equitable leaders become engaged leaders when they also nurture the three preconditions for equity in themselves—valuing difference, seeing the system, and using their power to redesign the system—and rewrite their own personal narratives about success.

Engaged and Equitable Leadership

3

Designing an organization where everyone thrives begins with engaged leadership. As discussed in the previous chapter, IDEA requires power brokers who can redesign systems and cultures; if leaders aren't on board, IDEA initiatives will be ineffective or inauthentic.

Engaged leaders are willing to use their power and influence to design a more equitable system so everyone has equal access to opportunity within their organizations. Equitable leadership requires going against established "best practices" at times, taking time to listen to others, and relentlessly questioning one's assumptions and beliefs. But first, equitable leaders must become comfortable with difference, seeing unity in diversity. When they do so, they begin to understand that great organizations encourage everyone to play to their strengths instead of insecurely asking everyone to fit into a mold of the "ideal" employee or leader.

In this chapter, we'll look at how leaders can nurture the first two preconditions of equity in themselves to become more equitable leaders. Then, in chapter 4, we'll explore how leaders can use their power to design a more equitable system.

Valuing Difference

Our brains are wired to feel threatened by difference. In *The Power Manual*, Suarez explains,

> The concept of difference is central to interactions in relationships of inequality. Humans have used differences to value, divide, and structure society—as with race, gender, class, age, and sexuality. One's relationship to difference impacts one's interactions, either reinforcing these structures of value or interrupting them.
>
> The supremacist approach to power offers two options for dealing with difference: ignore it or view it as cause for separation. A liberatory approach views differences as strengths and entertains interdependence as an option.[1]

How does one begin to nurture a liberatory approach to power? A number of researchers, especially Dr. Mitchell Hammer, president and founder of the Intercultural Development Inventory,[2] and Dr. Milton J. Bennett, creator of the Developmental Model of Intercultural Sensitivity,[3] have mapped a pathway from an ethnocentric or monocultural mindset to an ethnorelative or intercultural mindset (figure 4). This pathway offers a framework for growth for individuals seeking to enhance their ability to address and negotiate differences between and among individuals, groups, and cultures.

People with more monocultural mindsets either deny differences among groups or engage in polarization—an orientation in which they are either overly critical of other cultures or their own culture. As they progress toward an intercultural mindset, people begin to minimize differences, often repeating well-meaning phrases like

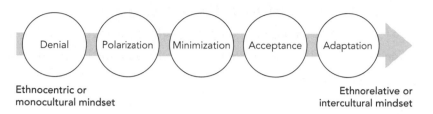

Ethnocentric or
monocultural mindset

Ethnorelative or
intercultural mindset

*Figure 4. Pathway from a monocultural to an intercultural mindset.
Adapted from Bennett (2017) and Hammer (2019).*

"We are more alike than different." The problem with this mindset is that it silences groups that are different and forces them to conform to dominant group characteristics.

Acceptance and adaptation mindsets require the courage to not be threatened by differences. A mindset of acceptance embraces cultural and group differences and asks how those differences can contribute to the collective good. People with adaptation mindsets alter their behavior according to their cultural context and abandon the notion that there is only one right way to do something. Many White Americans, for example, consider it right to be on time for everything. They quickly learn otherwise in other cultural contexts. If you're on time for an Indian wedding, for example, you'll be putting out chairs and helping set up the event. Being fashionably late is considered polite (unless you *want* to help set up, which is a good way to curry favor with aunties and uncles in the community). On the flip side, as I discovered when a college girlfriend got married, arriving thirty minutes late to a Protestant wedding means you will miss the entire ceremony. (Sorry, Liz and Rob!)

When leaders value difference, they are no longer threatened by peers or employees who think differently or disagree with them. They begin to understand that there is no one, singular truth when it comes to work but rather a kaleidoscope of perspectives. By taking the time to understand different perspectives, leaders can get a fuller picture of their marketplace, their competitors, and their future. In short, they can begin to see the system in which they operate in all its complexities.

System Sight

Equitable leaders are skilled at seeing systems and understanding interdependence. While valuing difference is the first step in the process of developing "system sight," leaders can hone their vision by understanding their own relationship to the systems they are in.

The tool Brevity & Wit uses to facilitate this understanding is the Group Identity Wheel, developed by DEI practitioners and executive coaches Sukari Pinnock-Fitts and Amber Mayes. The wheel positions your identity in relation to systems and power. Look at figure 5. (You can also download a copy of the Group Identity Wheel at www.TheEquityBook.com.) List your group identity for each dimension (race, age, gender, etc.) and mark whether each is a historically centered or marginalized group. You may find when you mark your identities and their saliency that some identities might not be easy to categorize. For example, I identify as a cisgender woman. Being a woman can be considered a marginalized identity but being cisgender places me in the center of most policies and systems. Embrace the paradoxes of your identity. The point of this exercise is to gain more awareness of the complexity of your identity, not to put yourself in a box.

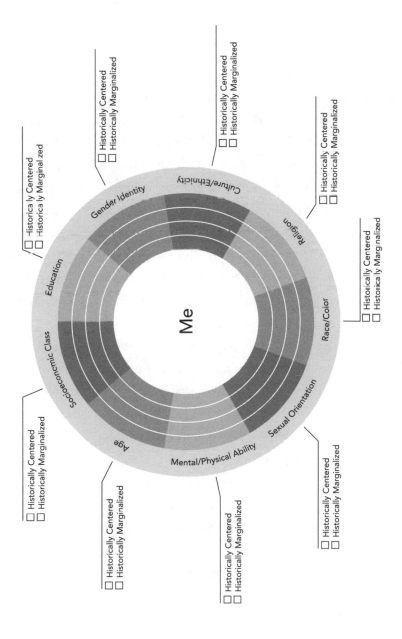

Figure 5. The Group Identity Wheel. © Fifth Domain Coaching. All rights reserved. Not to be reproduced without express permission of Sukari Pinnock-Fitts and Amber Mayes. For more info, visit http://www.fifthdomaincoaching.com.

Within the wheel (center): Me

Segments around wheel:
- Gender Identity
- Culture/Ethnicity
- Education
- Religion
- Socioeconomic Class
- Race/Color
- Age
- Sexual Orientation
- Mental/Physical Ability

Checkbox labels around wheel:
- ☐ Historically Centered ☐ Historically Marginalized

In figure 6, I colored in the wheel according to the saliency of each dimension of my identity; that is, I shaded each "spoke" of the wheel according to how much I thought about that aspect of my identity as I move through the world. How cognizant am I of my race or gender or mental and physical ability as I go to work, run errands, or hang out with friends? You should ask yourself the same, indicating which dimensions resonate most with you. In other words, how often are these dimensions of your identity top of mind as you go about your day? This might change according to the various spheres of life. For example, your age might be marginalized at work if you are over sixty-five and highly salient for you there but irrelevant when you interact with your neighbors. However, because you likely spend more hours at work than talking with your neighbors, I recommend coloring in the wheel according to how you spend most of your day; doing so will help you see which dimensions of identity are most front and center as you move through the world.

By illustrating your marginalization *and* your privilege, this exercise can help you better understand the relationship between dimensions of your identity and the systems you participate in. People usually find that their most marginalized identities are those that are most salient to them. This is understandable; if you are in a minority, you likely face more threats to your physical and psychological safety because most people have been conditioned to fear difference. Being aware of the dimensions of your identity that are marginalized is a protective factor. For me, my ethnicity is most salient because it distinguishes me not only from the majority of the US population but also from the majority of the Indian American community. Few Indian Americans are familiar with Coorg, my father's homeland, and because my mother is Punjabi and not from Coorg, I have faced exclusion in the Coorg community as well.

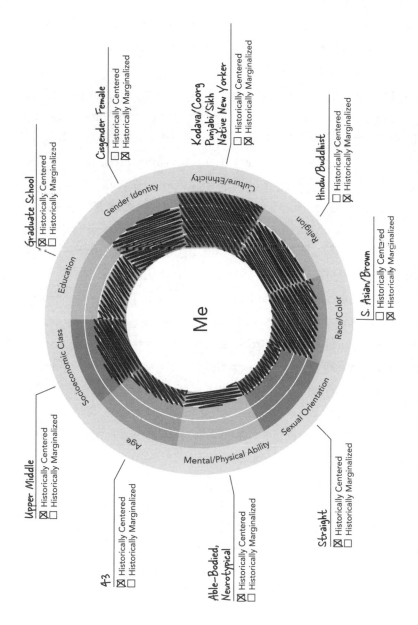

The following labels appear around the wheel diagram:

Graduate School
☒ Historically Centered
☐ Historically Marginalized

Cisgender Female
☐ Historically Centered
☒ Historically Marginalized

**Kodava/Coorg
Punjabi/Sikh
Native New Yorker**
☐ Historically Centered
☒ Historically Marginalized

Hindu/Buddhist
☐ Historically Centered
☒ Historically Marginalized

S. Asian/Brown
☐ Historically Centered
☒ Historically Marginalized

Straight
☒ Historically Centered
☐ Historically Marginalized

**Able-Bodied,
Neurotypical**
☒ Historically Centered
☐ Historically Marginalized

43
☒ Historically Centered
☐ Historically Marginalized

Upper Middle
☒ Historically Centered
☐ Historically Marginalized

Wheel segment labels: Gender Identity, Culture/Ethnicity, Education, Religion, Socioeconomic Class, Race/Color, Age, Sexual Orientation, Mental/Physical Ability. Center: **Me**

Figure 6. Minal's group identities. © Fifth Domain Coaching. All rights reserved. Not to be reproduced without express permission of Sukari Pinnock-Fitts and Amber Mayes. For more info, visit http://www.fifthdomaincoaching.com.

But you should also examine dimensions of identity that are historically centered, asking yourself, "How does the system support me and others with this identity?" For me, I must constantly remind myself of my privilege as a straight, cisgender individual and question whether a system or policy is considering the needs of others without that privilege. I also know that, generally speaking, Indian women enjoy a rather positive stereotype in the workplace of being intelligent. This means I don't have to credential myself when speaking or giving my opinion the way other women of color might have to. Understanding both your marginalization and your privilege is vital to being an engaged and equitable leader. And if I am interested in being an ally to people without the same level of privilege, then I must ask myself, "How can I lift up the voices that may be struggling to be heard over mine in this organization?"

You should also ask yourself questions about how your identity might be perceived by others and how you may need to account for perception regardless of the truth, as you move through the world. For example, as a Brown and South Asian woman, I have sometimes been mistaken for being Muslim and subjected to Islamophobia. While my gut reaction might be to correct someone about their misperception, I have trained myself not to respond in such a manner because doing so may implicitly reinforce that it's okay to be Islamophobic. Instead, my response is to let people think I'm Muslim and address their bias against Muslims. Similarly, White people who may think of themselves more along the lines of their ethnicity (Italian, Irish, etc.) and/or class (Southern poor, lower class, etc.) still need to be aware of the world's perception of them as White and hold themselves accountable for the privilege that entails.

Finally, it's important for you to understand how a change in a dimension of identity may require you to change your understanding of yourself and your behavior. Just ten years ago, I was making less than $45,000 while living in New York City, which felt like lower middle-class given the high cost of living of the area. (Indeed, living independently in a one-bedroom apartment was out of the question at that income level.) Today, I am in a higher income bracket in an area with a slightly lower cost of living, but many of the behaviors and attitudes I adopted from those days of scraping by have not left me. And because of that, I may be blind to the financial privilege I now enjoy. It is incredibly uncomfortable for me to think of myself as upper middle-class and even more uncomfortable for me to share that with others. But ignoring, erasing, or trying to change that fact makes me a poor role model for the courageous conversations we need to have about identity and privilege if we really want to design a more equitable world.

Equity in Personal Storytelling

One of the capstone practices in equitable leadership involves rewriting your story of success. As discussed more fully in chapter 5, social scientists have found that the most pernicious barrier to IDEA is the myth of the self-made man, also known as rugged individualism. This myth is so pernicious and widespread in US society and beyond that our minds automatically attribute disparate outcomes between groups to individual effort. We can't see how systems support some people's success but not others' because we have bought so completely into the myth that we all go it alone.

This idea shapes how we tell stories. The Hero's Journey, a monomyth made famous by cultural and religious scholar Joseph Campbell, is the template used to shape narratives in many books and movies. It involves a protagonist who goes on an adventure, experiences a crisis, overcomes it, and then returns home transformed. Everyone from Pixar cartoonists to nonprofit fundraising professionals has been influenced by this template.

The Hero's Journey certainly holds people's attention. But it also makes the system invisible and silent, thereby reinforcing oppressive behaviors and protecting those in power.

Equitable leaders are willing to break the silence and become transparent about the system, their privilege, and the support they received from others in their story of success. I often tell people that they are not ready to address IDEA until they can talk about their privilege and victimization in the same breath. Everyone I have ever known has some experience with both. The scales may tip toward one over the other, but I have never met anyone who has not experienced some type of privilege and some type of marginalization.

Sometimes, people with dominant identities attribute their success to luck. I've observed this most often in White men who identify as politically progressive. But let me be clear: crediting luck—no matter how humble your intentions—does not help. In fact, it reinforces oppression because it obscures the system, making it impossible for people with marginalized identities to understand its rules and design their lives for success within it. If you really want to advance equity, tell your story of success by highlighting how the system either supports you or is designed to support you. Doing so won't make you a braggart; rather, storytelling of this nature conveys a deeper sense of humility when done well.

For example, someone at a client organization once complimented me on the success of Brevity & Wit, which grew exponentially between 2019 and 2020.

"It must be hard to start a business. And impressive that you've been able to make it so successful," she said.

"Yeah," I replied. "But it wouldn't have happened if I hadn't gotten married."

She looked surprised, no doubt because she knows I'm a fiery feminist and that my husband has little to do with my work. But I pressed on.

"I tried to go out on my own multiple times when I was single," I explained. "But I couldn't make it work between paying for health insurance and earning enough to live on. Getting on my husband's health insurance and having his income as a buffer made it possible. It wasn't a huge buffer—I had to turn a profit within a few months— but it was enough and more than I ever had when I was single."

The client, a single mother, looked relieved and seemed to appreciate my candor. It was clear I was not going to perpetuate the myth of the "alley cat" entrepreneur who scrapes by no matter the circumstances, while "house cats" take safe jobs with benefits. By talking about the external support I've received, I demystified my success and, hopefully, helped build a bridge across difference.

What Does Engaged Leadership Look Like?

In 2020, Brevity & Wit worked with Evans Consulting, a boutique firm dedicated to cocreating healthy organizations. Early on, founder Sue Evans established a commitment to a human-centered culture and a spirit of servant leadership. Yet, while the company scores high on measures of inclusion and was named a top workplace by the *Washington Post*,[4] it lacks diversity, particularly racial diversity.

Since its inception, Evans has had an apolitical culture; leaders and employees rarely talk about politics, race, religion, or other "controversial" topics. In early 2020, the leadership team, headed by managing partners and owners Jack Moore and Bob Etris, began preliminary talks about DEI, work that intensified after the murder of George Floyd in May of that year. I was working as Evans's part-time chief marketing officer and used my dual knowledge in communications and IDEA to help the company respond to widespread calls for racial justice. I will never forget what Jack said to me during those heavy, urgent days as we sought to expand my role to support them on IDEA: "I don't want to just put out a toothless statement; I want to do the hard work."

There is no debating the fact that fostering equity in an organization is hard work that takes courage and self-reflection; it's also just and moral and well worth any leader's time. I will forever feel that it was my privilege to work with two straight, White men who were relentlessly brave in how they approached this work; it certainly isn't the norm.

For the rest of 2020 and into 2021, Jack and Bob carved out time every week to work on IDEA, and they listened to both experts and staff members. Each week, I had a one-hour call with them and Nicole Anderson, the company's director of people, who also displayed exceptional openness and courage during this process. Nicole led the creation of a DEIA Council tasked with developing a strategy to advise leaders. Jack and Bob asked Brevity & Wit to assess the organization and did not get defensive in response to tough feedback, such as when we reported a pervasive culture of conflict avoidance within the organization. They immediately began to implement our recommendations, such as establishing a salary floor for all new positions, a tactic that ensures every employee needs only one job to live a middle-class life. They also began to take steps to advance equity independent of my counsel. For most of 2020, they had been informally reaching out to their networks to recruit for a new leadership position. As it became clear that Evans's lack of racial diversity was likely due to a reliance on referrals for recruitment, Jack and Bob paused all discussions about the position until a job description was posted and a diverse candidate pool could be recruited.

We worked through many of the tools described above, and at an annual company retreat (held virtually due to COVID-19), Bob and Jack both shared their professional journeys with employees, noting how the system was built for two straight, White guys like them. Bob went first:

> I grew up in a household and in a community where the underlying thought was, if you worked hard and followed the rules and did everything that you could through school, then success would follow. And as I got into the work world, and as I took on, you know, different areas of responsibility, I tried to model behavior of different leaders that I respected and tried to learn from the behavior of different leaders I couldn't stand, under the guise of, if you just try to be the boss that you always wanted to have, then you can do right by people and you'll be in a good place.
>
> And some elements of that may be true. But in stepping back and really taking a different look at the world really triggered by the events of this year, it's fair to say that the rules are not set up in a fair way. And in some ways, the rules of how society works, how education works, how some aspects of government work, and even some things within Evans could stand to be more fair.
>
> And it's really with that recognition in mind that Jack and I decided that we really needed to accelerate what we were doing.

I know I have on multiple occasions talked about how diversity and inclusion can be a hard thing to talk about. It can make people uncomfortable. It can make me uncomfortable. It's new. It's not easy for everyone. I think it's important that we all start talking differently about how it's the right thing to do. And it's the moral thing to do. And it's the responsible thing to do. And those are wonderful feelings, and it can help remove some of that discomfort with the newness for those of us for whom this is a newer topic.

Then Jack brought it home with a message that centered both courage and vulnerability:

You know, right after George Floyd's murder, I remember being told in our Monday leadership call that I needed to—that Bob and I needed to—establish a voice on racism. And in that early video I shared with you all, you may remember that I was taught growing up that I shouldn't get involved in racism, that it wasn't my business and I should shut the heck up. And, we all know, I'm very conflict-averse, so guidance like that is, you know—it feels like a blessing. This journey has been a wake-up call. And it started in that leadership team call on that Monday. But eventually, I realized it was driven by all of you. And I started paying attention to things that I hadn't before, and what it did was it opened my eyes that the things that seemed new weren't. They've been going on around me my whole life. And I made a choice, a long time ago, that was fueled by privilege, a lot of naïveté, and fear.

One of the key qualities of Evans is to look deeper, to ask why. And to not be okay with just dealing with symptoms.

And so, my position was, well, it was dripping with irony. Bob shared his comments with me last night, and I couldn't agree more with the idea that this is the just, the right, the moral, the responsible thing to do. And for me that means continuing to learn and asking why and digging deeper and, like I said a minute ago, experiencing some failure. But not being afraid to take action.

And underneath all that—like if you've been listening and wondering, "Okay, has he really said what his *why* is at this point?"—it's because we expect a lot from you, and you have the right to expect that, and even more, from us. Our culture is pretty good. But it can be better. And I think working together we can accomplish that. We can make it even better. And it's because you guys deserve it. So thank you.

If you are a straight, White man struggling to figure out what to do in this new world of equity and racial justice, then the pithiest advice I have for you is this: be like Jack and Bob. Don't wait for conditions to be perfect to try; be vulnerable and brave; and put your people before your ego.

Oh, and listen to me and other women of color in your orbit. We give great advice and feedback.

Bridging the Gap

If you're willing to embrace difference and have some ability to see systems and your relation to them, you can begin to design your organization—the system you have the most power to influence—in a way that promotes equity and greater opportunity for all, as illustrated in our theory of change (see figure 2 in chapter 1). To best show how to do this, we'll walk through a case study with NPR and explore how other organizations are prototyping solutions that expand IDEA beyond the realm of human resources.

Engaged leaders understand that if they want to design more equitable organizations, they need to center people who have historically been pushed to the margins. This begins with the empathic practice of perspective-gathering, where leaders take time either formally (through assessments) or informally (through feedback and conversation) to listen to the experiences and needs of people on the margins. This is a good time to tap **employee resource groups (ERGs)**, if you have them, or hold listening tours, where you invite all or representative individuals of your organization to share their thoughts with you.

Using the data gathered from these steps, as well as from conversations with leaders and other power brokers in the organization, you can begin to define equitable outcomes. These could be traditional IDEA goals, like a greater percentage of people of color in leadership positions, or something unique, like finding a way to compensate staff members who are known IDEA resources in the organization because they do the labor of educating peers or answer those "Got a minute?" questions about language in marketing collateral or some new report.

Defining Equitable Outcomes

Equitable outcomes should aim for long-term improvement and are usually more ambitious than the observable behaviors we'll define later. For example, when I worked with NPR, the newsroom was working to diversify news sources across all its shows. Data had shown a significant drop in source diversity in recent years, and the head of news had set a goal to at least return to the previous high-water mark, where 73 percent of sources were White and 27 percent were people of color. This outcome was clearly measurable, but news mangers did not have a clear pathway to get there.

Observable behaviors are your pathway—the bridge between awareness and impact. At NPR, we needed to break down the critical moves needed to reach the desired outcome. Through multiple conversations, I encouraged news managers to focus on one change for the year. After perspective-gathering and input from power brokers like Keith Woods, NPR's chief diversity officer, and Nancy Brand, NPR's senior vice president of news, we agreed that the observable behavior should be that "by the end of 2020, every journalist is tracking source diversity."

My work with NPR was unconventional because I met with news managers for only one hour every few weeks. Most IDEA consultants allocate half- or full-day sessions to brainstorming solutions.

But given the demanding nature of my client's work, which included covering the chaotic Trump administration, I understandably couldn't get more than an hour of their time in any given week. Good designers are flexible and put end users at the center of the design process, so I adjusted accordingly.

However, the time limitation also meant that any solution—even if people had enough motivation and clear direction—was going to face some resistance. News managers are under constant deadline pressure; to describe their jobs as busy and time-crunched is an understatement. As the Heath brothers write, "What looks like laziness is often exhaustion."[1] I turned to Keith and to Sara Richards, an NPR project manager, who helped identify and recruit news managers who were already tracking sources. We asked those news managers to present their methods to the group during one of our lunchtime meetings—a way of prototyping multiple solutions and highlighting "bright spots," as the Heath brothers call them—areas in the system where things are going right despite the existing obstacles.[2] One manager shared a spreadsheet he was using to track sources, while another played a clip of her asking a source about his gender and racial identity. Another manager explained how she tracked this information in Slack after her segments aired. We then made these diverse tools available to all managers via email so that other news managers could quickly mimic and adopt the behavior we wanted to see in the organization. The diversity of tools is important because it conveyed a fundamental aspect of equitable design: no solitary solution works for everyone. Because variety was introduced into solutions, employees were able to select what worked for them and were given implicit permission to create something new.

These efforts paid off quickly. Within a month, Keith received an email from a news manager saying, "While at first I was skeptical of the merits of tracking, I was quickly able to see trends and patterns as I kept this data. That was more helpful to me than I anticipated in real time. Seeing the data in this format versus looking at the rundown everyday definitely made a difference personally in seeing how the show broke down along these lines [of diversity]."

Bake Behaviors into Systems

Observable behaviors are critical in designing organizations where everyone can thrive, but they are not enough. You must make sure that the organization's system and processes reinforce desired behaviors and, if possible, do so invisibly.

Early in my engagement with NPR, I led news managers through an exercise in which they broke into groups and discussed obstacles that could get in the way of diversifying sources. In lieu of sticky notes, they documented their ideas on flip chart paper, which we collected and then shared in a follow-up meeting via email and a slide presentation. Through discussion and perspective sharing, we all realized that the culture of the newsroom could be hindering efforts to diversify sources. A strong emphasis on meeting deadlines above all else served to discourage some reporters and producers from finding sources different from the ones they already had. In other words, if reporters are rewarded for filing on time above all else, they are disincentivized to take the time to find and vet diverse sources. This lack of system reinforcement was undermining diversity efforts; indeed, human nature is such that most people will prioritize security (e.g., keeping a job) over risk (e.g., trying something new).

When this came to light, I spoke with Keith and Nancy again, this time about amending NPR's performance review process and holding news managers accountable for tracking sources. We spoke about the various options available to them, such as making it an explicitly required behavior, or tying compensation and bonuses to it. The organization was in the midst of making those changes as this book went to print, and these reinforcing structures will help nudge the system toward greater equity. At the same time, Keith invited me back to speak with the entire editorial staff about creating more equitable content using the REACH equity content screen (which we'll dive into in chapter 6); doing so helped increase the pressure on news managers because the staff was now galvanized by a public commitment to greater equity in content creation.

NPR's challenges around system reinforcement are not unique; many organizations have systems and processes that undermine IDEA efforts. Think of company leaders who claim they want to recruit more women but offer frat-house-style perks like foosball tables and kegs, which reinforce male-centric cultures. Or consider leaders who are trying to create a harassment-free environment but adhere to open floor plans, which research shows leave women (and likely nonbinary folk as well) feeling more watched and observed, and thus, more vulnerable to harassment.[3]

Often, equitable solutions depend on context. In recent decades, orchestras began holding blind auditions, where applicants perform behind screens. Between 1970 and 1997, the percent of female musicians in the nation's top five symphony orchestras soared from less than 5 percent to 25 percent.[4] Corporate leaders adopted this idea and began erasing identifying information in résumés in job databases, a practice called résumé screening. However, while blind auditions can effectively diversify orchestras, research shows that résumé screening has had mixed results in corporations and is now generally discouraged.[5] One reason is because a candidate's race eventually comes to light, and if the organization has not done its work around mitigating bias, a blind interview process is not a sufficient solution for exclusion and inequity. Another reason is because résumé screening for corporate jobs is not a step toward equity so much as an erasure of an important part of identity that may influence how candidates do their job or the experience and expertise they bring to the organization.

That doesn't mean you shouldn't try new things to advance equity. For example, when I worked with NPR's editorial staff on applying an equity lens to news coverage and programming, I delivered a series of recorded webinars on the subject. One power broker later wrote to Keith, "Because our newscast schedules are all over the map, I am hoping most of them [the journalists] will take in the recordings. As added incentive, we are paying anyone who does the sessions live or invests the time to watch the recordings outside of their shifts—so they can include their time spent participating on their time sheets."

Don't be afraid to use your power and influence, however small or large it is, to close the gaps in your organization.

Nudging

A **nudge** is a way of presenting choices that encourage people to choose the option in their best interest while preserving their ability to opt out. In other words, it nudges people in one direction (toward IDEA) but preserves their right to free choice.

If you can, you want to design systems and processes so that engaging in inclusive and equitable behavior is almost unconscious.

Novelty is great for motivating change but terrible for sustaining it. For example, in 2009, designers created the Piano Stairs at a subway station in Stockholm, Sweden. Each step was a piano key that made a sound when stepped on. The idea was to nudge commuters to improve their health by walking up the stairs instead of riding the escalator. A YouTube video shows commuters happily "playing" the stairs when they were first installed.

But the fun lasted for only a couple of days, notes Christina Gravert, a behavioral economist at the University of Copenhagen. "The initial excitement of your very own Tom Hanks–style dance from the movie *Big* must have quickly given way to the reality of rush hour, as commuters trampled over keys going up and down the stairs," she writes. "To no surprise, the piano disappeared."[6]

The folly of novelty is also evident in the field of international development. Well-intentioned designers developed the PlayPump to bring drinking water to communities in several African countries by harnessing the power of play. The device used energy created by children playing on a merry-go-round to fill a water tank. Hailed as "ingenious,"[7] the PlayPump attracted major media attention and drew support from the likes of former first lady Laura Bush and AOL founder Steve Case.

But after a few years and millions in funding, many PlayPumps sit idle, and hand pumps have been reinstalled to serve the community.[8]

What happened?

WaterAid, an international nonprofit organization, criticized the PlayPump "as being far too expensive, too complex for local maintenance, overreliant on child labour, and based on flawed water demand calculations," according to an article in the *Guardian*.[9] From a design perspective, the problem seems to have been flawed from the start. First, the creators did not involve any African children or

mothers in the design. Trevor Field was a White advertising executive who lived in the United Kingdom and licensed the design for
a PlayPump from Ronnie Stuiver, a South Africa–based borehole
driller and engineer. Both men promoted a design and invention
that required low-income African children to spend their time
"playing" to access clean drinking water. (Play, by definition, is pur-
poseless. If you are doing something for the purpose of deriving an
essential need for survival, it is not play; it is work.) When African
mothers rightfully sent their children to school instead, the mothers
had to use the merry-go-round themselves to get drinking water,
evoking a mental imge of indignity that makes me cringe.

The PlayPump hinged on novelty. It was the Piano Stairs all over
again but much worse because it compromised women's dignity in
their pursuit of drinking water, a basic human right. Humanitarian
aid and global development are nearing sixty years of operation in
low-income countries, and aid organizations can no longer afford
to treat Africa like a tinkering shed. Equity means seeing all Africans
as worthy of sustainable, cocreated innovations that work in their
context and meet their specific needs.

So how do you make your designed solutions sustainable? Through
invisibility. And nudging can help create invisible solutions without
taking away an individual's right to choice.

An organizational nudge toward equity or inclusion might look
like hospital rooms with the names of patients displayed clearly on
whiteboards so all medical staff can address them by name, thereby
rehumanizing them. Or it might look like an onboarding process
that automatically opts new employees in to your implicit bias training (but also lets them opt out; mandatory trainings are known
to backfire). Or it could be video conference software that adds

people's pronouns to their display names. (*The Inclusion Nudges Guidebook* by Lisa Kepinski and Tinna C. Nielsen is full of other nudges to create more inclusive and equitable environments.) In short, a good nudge is invisible, preserves choice, and reduces the mental bandwidth required to engage in inclusive and equitable behaviors. Of those three factors, invisibility is the most critical if you want to create *sustainable* change and ensure your organization is equitable in the long run.

Technology and Equity

The opposite of a nudge is a **dark pattern**. Dark patterns, a term coined by Harry Brignull, an expert in user experience design, are features of websites and mobile apps that trick users into doing things they may not want to do but that benefit the business behind the product and disguise or eliminate user choice.[10] Because this term reinforces colorist biases associating darkness with badness, I will use the term **unethical pattern** going forward. I included the original name for those who are interested in learning more about this practice and how to avoid it.

Unethical patterns are ubiquitous these days. Try closing your account with Amazon. In fact, just try finding the link to get information about closing your account. You'd think it would be under the "Your Account" tab. It's not. Instead, you have to scroll to the bottom right corner of the page, click "Help," and then scroll down to "Managing Your Account." Then, as you hover over that option, you'll see an option to "Request the Closure of Your Account and the Deletion of Your Personal Information." You'll be taken to a page that offers information on closing your account but then asks you to click on "Close Your Amazon Account" to get to the actual page, where you finally have the option to review all the services Amazon controls (Amazon Prime, Whole Foods membership rewards, etc.). Then, finally, at the bottom of a long page, you can choose your reason to close your account and click "Close My Account."

This is an unethical pattern because it causes people to give up on closing their accounts out of emotional attrition rather than a change in decision. Another example is hiding an unsubscribe link to an email newsletter by changing the text color from the default blue to the color of the copy near the hyperlink.

Technology is a major part of any organization and therefore plays a major role in creating more equitable relationships with both employees and customers. Unethical patterns like these prevent customers from engaging on fair terms. Organizations committed to equity should mitigate these types of practices whenever possible.

The problem is that most of us think data and technology are inherently unbiased—that they're just cold numbers or inert algorithms operating without human emotion. But the truth is that technology is coded by humans and data is gathered by humans, with their myriad biases.

When companies use artificial intelligence (AI) or machine learning to score job applications, the results can unfairly favor certain groups. If algorithms are meant to predict candidates who will do well at an organization, then they may select candidates who are similar to those who have been promoted at the organization in the past. If that happens to be predominantly White men, then algorithms will continue to select White male candidates. Even if algorithms mask names and identifying characteristics, they will favor proxy categories for Whiteness and maleness, such as "people who played rugby in college."[11]

This problem is so pervasive that researchers from Google's AI research company, DeepMind, and the University of Oxford recently recommended that AI practitioners draw on **anticolonial theory** to "reform the industry, put ethical principles into practice, and avoid further algorithmic exploitation or oppression," according to an article in *VentureBeat*, a publication that covers the tech industry.[12] To turn AI ethical principles into practice, researchers from Google, Intel, OpenAI, and other top research labs advise paying developers to find bias in AI systems—a recommendation that *VentureBeat* compares to bounties offered to hackers who find bugs in security software.[13]

Debiasing technology could be the subject of its own book. I mention it here because technology is the backbone of all organizations these days—especially after the pandemic forced many of us to work from home for extended periods. Any organization looking to put equity front and center must take a mindful approach to selecting, designing, and redesigning its technological infrastructure.

Of course, none of these strategies will be effective if you can't rally your crowd around the change. In the next chapter, we'll discuss how to use behavior change communications to more effectively motivate your team, department, or organization to implement IDEA initiatives.

Communicating the Change

When it comes to scaling IDEA across an organization, designing effective communications to help generate buy-in is critical, just as it is in any change management process. In this chapter, we'll draw on lessons from psychology, anthropology, and other disciplines to give you the tools you need to effectively align and move your organization toward greater inclusion, diversity, equity, and accessibility. But first, a short word on language and grammar.

If Race Is Language, Caste Is Grammar

Isabel Wilkerson's book *Caste: The Origins of Our Discontents* is an x-ray of inequality around the world, illuminating the bones of the system. "If we have been trained to see humans in the language of race, then caste is the underlying grammar that we encode as children, as when learning our mother tongue," she writes. "Caste, like grammar, becomes an invisible guide not only to how we speak, but to how we process information. . . . Many of us have never taken a class in grammar, yet we know in our bones that a transitive verb takes an object, that a subject needs a predicate."[1]

Wilkerson's metaphor also applies very literally to communications for IDEA, as the work of mitigating bias is often about recoding the grammar of our thought processes. Sometimes, to be good inclusion allies, clients ask Brevity & Wit for a list of inclusive terms. We do not provide one, first, because terms are evolving, and second, because word choice is secondary to sentence construction, the grammar of how one *thinks* about different groups.

Some Indian immigrants, for example, use offensive terms like "Red Indians" when referring to Native Americans because this was how they were taught to distinguish themselves from Indigenous peoples of North America. But their speech is often along the lines of "What White people did to Red Indians is criminal. They clearly committed genocide."

Their word choice is wrong, but their grammar—the sentence construction and the thinking behind it—is spot on. Word choice should be corrected but not in a way that invalidates the larger idea. On the flip side, remember Amy Cooper, the White woman who told an innocent bird-watcher who asked her to put her dog on a leash that she was going to call the police "to tell them there's an African American man threatening my life" in Central Park?[2] She used the right terms, but her sentence structure reflected racist ideology. The grammar of her sentence upheld the terror of White supremacy over Black men.

This is why I am rather flexible about whether we use the term IDEA or DEI or diversity and inclusion. On one level, words matter immensely because they bring visibility and respect to marginalized people. But on a deeper level, the structure of your sentences, which reflects the structure of your thoughts, matters more. (This does not mean you should abandon all efforts to get word choice right. I am giving you permission to abandon perfection for earnest effort. I am not giving you permission to half-ass this.)

Keep the grammar of your thinking top of mind as we explore how to construct communications that advance IDEA in your organization.

Behavior Change Communications

Behavior change communications has been an effective tool in enacting many public health policies, such as advocacy efforts designed to increase condom use to prevent HIV/AIDS or campaigns that helped make school meals more nutritious. Since behaviors are our bridge to more equitable organizations, it behooves us to pull from this well-researched field to help us transform our organizations.

Behavior change communications, just like behavior change management, asks us to first identify obstacles to getting people to adopt new behaviors. According to Sabine Marx, Brevity & Wit's communications strategist, organizations face predictable obstacles. One obstacle is risk perception, which is very subjective. If people think they aren't at risk of being affected by an issue or event (such as a disease, a natural disaster, or racial injustice), they aren't likely to take protective action for themselves or their organization. Another obstacle is the shortcuts our minds naturally take when processing information; we may trust what *sounds* true over what *is* true because the former aligns with our existing ideas about the world. A third obstacle is low motivation. Indeed, if people were motivated by information alone, we would all floss every night, exercise regularly, and avoid credit card debt. A fourth barrier is the perception that there is no solution, which can lead to denying the existence of the problem and an attitude of "why bother?"

Fortunately, **framing** helps break through this resistance. A message frame organizes and structures a message without altering its arguments or attributes. Researchers have found that the same message with the same data framed in different ways has different persuasive effects. The Center for Research on Environmental Decisions (CRED) at Columbia University (where Sabine served as a research scientist for more than ten years) found that people prefer the term "carbon offset" to "carbon tax" when evaluating climate change solutions, even though both terms represent a surcharge whose revenue would be used to fund the same program. Interestingly, the frame effect hinged on people's political affiliations. Liberals were equally likely to support a program to increase the cost of products that contribute significantly to climate change, regardless of the term used. Conservatives, however, were more likely to support the program if the term "carbon offset" was used to describe it.[3]

Framing is not intended to deceive or manipulate people but rather to make complex ideas more accessible. Frames help build public trust.

The FrameWorks Institute is a nonprofit think tank that researches how to frame policy issues for public discourse. In 2009, Frame-Works released a brief entitled *Talking about Disparities: The Effect of Frame Choices on Support for Race-Based Policies* that examines how to frame racial equity. Summarizing extensive research on how Americans think and talk about race, the brief details effective frames for addressing racial disparities in education, housing, health care, and other social issues.[4] (While IDEA encompasses more than racial diversity, race is often the most polarizing type of diversity in this work and is therefore a good place to start in developing unifying messaging. As we'll see, effective frames around race do not prohibit the inclusion of other dimensions of diversity.)

The researchers listed three obstacles to talking about systemic racism in the United States, which I have summarized as

- The *progress and personalization* narrative
- The belief in *rugged individualism*
- The *separate fates* narrative

The progress and personalization narrative rests on the widespread belief that racial matters have improved dramatically in the sixty years since the passage of the Civil Rights Act and that the racism that still exists is primarily at an individual level. This feeds into rugged individualism, the belief that one's success or failure in life is solely constructed by one's own effort. This belief poses the biggest obstacle to IDEA work because it is so pervasive, particularly when it comes to work and money. Because of their belief in rugged individualism, White people often attribute certain life outcomes, such as low levels of education and wealth, to a failure to embody the values associated with rugged individualism, such as agency and hard work. However, they don't see the corollary—that people who exhibit agency and hard work still suffer and live in poverty.

As we saw earlier, and hopefully as you learned when rewriting your story of success, no one is an island. We are all interdependent; our success depends on many causes and conditions. But a belief in rugged individualism leads to the separate fates narrative, the idea that what happens to one person or group doesn't affect us. This makes it easy to classify someone as the "other" and eventually leads to segregation and dehumanization.

Fortunately, FrameWorks found that frames that focus on shared values transcend these beliefs and narratives. Values-based framing helps unify people before they dive into discussions of race and helps reduce defensiveness and resistance. Three frames are particularly powerful in framing IDEA in organizations:[5]

1. *Ingenuity/solutions first.* US culture prizes ingenuity and innovation so much that people will transcend concerns about race. This frame leads with solutions whenever possible and emphasizes that society should use more innovation and ingenuity to create programs and services that benefit communities.

2. *Opportunity for all.* There was consistent support for a frame that promotes the value of equal opportunity for all. Opportunity is the amount of access people have to societal resources and is dependent on how the system is set up to distribute those resources. As FrameWorks' research states, "People are able to acknowledge that there are many places where the system falls down. Insofar as we could show systemic breakdowns that left certain populations behind, we were able to move people to think about racial inequality in a fundamentally different and more productive way."

3. *Interdependence.* The reality of interdependence, when made visible, allows people to see the promotion of justice and equity as critical to the common good. Talking about how we all depend on each other allows us to picture our shared fates. It also tends to lead to more brainstorming around solutions.

Speaking to the shared values of ingenuity/solutions first, opportunity for all, and interdependence is a positive and effective way to unite an organization around a common cause. Some of the most effective change agents have intuitively understood this, such as Rev. Martin Luther King Jr., who famously used a frame of interdependence to inspire Americans to action: "We are caught in an inescapable network of mutuality, tied in a single garment of destiny. Whatever affects one directly, affects all indirectly."[6]

However, finding common values does *not* mean we should devalue difference. Remember the pathway from a monocultural to an intercultural mindset (figure 4)? We don't want to allow our desire to unify an organization around a shared vision to conflict with the need to recognize, discuss, and embrace differences. But we do need to frame communications in a way that makes talking about differences less threatening so we can bring these values to life.

This framing technique can be used for both internal and external messaging and should absolutely be used when launching IDEA initiatives. In fact, its threads are evident in the remarks by Jack and Bob of Evans Consulting at the end of chapter 3. But for an IDEA frame to be effective, it needs to explain how the system leads to inequitable outcomes.

The *how* is crucial. Too often, people blindly believe or reject statements about race, whether the message is "Racism is systemic" or "White people have privilege." Such blanket statements are poor communication devices for inclusion; they do more to divide than to unite across difference because they assume a knowledge of the system or privilege that most people don't have. If we want to make such statements, we must first explain the how behind them. How are White people privileged? Do we mean that White supremacist thought has infected us all, regardless of skin color, and all White people benefit from this ideology? If that's true, then how do they benefit? And how do they benefit in your organization? You need to explain the causal links between ways of thinking and the results we see in our organizations and the world around us. Here's an example:

The average white-collar job was created in the 1950s and designed for White men, many of whom had wives who managed the emotional and cognitive labor of a household for free. Because salaries have not kept up with inflation, most households now need two incomes to live middle-class lives, and there is more emotional and cognitive labor than before. Women still shoulder the majority of this work but now on the margins of their jobs. The nine-to-five workday, where employees drive to work from the suburbs and return home to a healthy, homemade dinner prepared by someone else, and where a single income can cover the cost of a mortgage, retirement, and college tuition, is no longer a reality. It's no wonder that most employees—male, female, and nonbinary—feel more stress, are in poorer health, and experience more financial insecurity than their 1950s counterparts. How might we redesign work so that it supports health, well-being, and financial prosperity for all members of a household?

Targeted Messaging

Targeted messaging is different from framing in that it has a certain audience and behavior in mind. In other words, framing shapes the discourse, and targeted messaging moves individuals to action.

Spitfire Strategies is a communications firm that supports nonprofit organizations and foundations in communications for social change. Its Smart Chart blueprint coaches change agents to identify their target audiences' values and the barriers to the change they want to see before crafting targeted messages.[7] The Smart Chart then provides a message box, a tool to develop a concise, values-based message that can win over target audiences (see figure 7). The message box includes four parts to a good message: a *top value* that is shared between the messenger and the target audience; a *barrier breaker*, which has the power to break through a target audience's known resistance; a clear *ask*, which is a tangible action the target audience can take; and an *echo vision*, which is a reminder of what the world will look like when change is realized.

Because of Spitfire's generosity in sharing its tools, Brevity & Wit has used the message box as inspiration for a message template for IDEA communications (figure 8). IDEA communications need a linear template, one that starts with identifying values and barriers and then provides an explanatory model by outlining the why, how, and what to form the causal link discussed earlier. Without this explanatory model, communications about the disparities between any two groups are likely to be attributed to individual agency instead of systemic causes. The why and how correlate to the barrier breaker message in the Spitfire message box, while the what correlates to

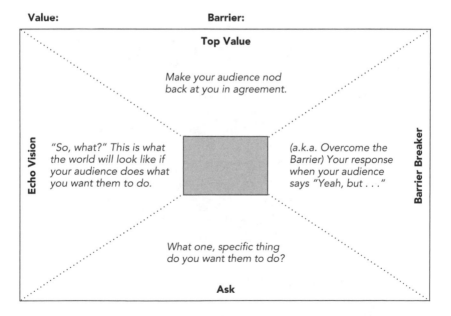

Figure 7. Spitfire Strategies' message box. © Spitfire Strategies.

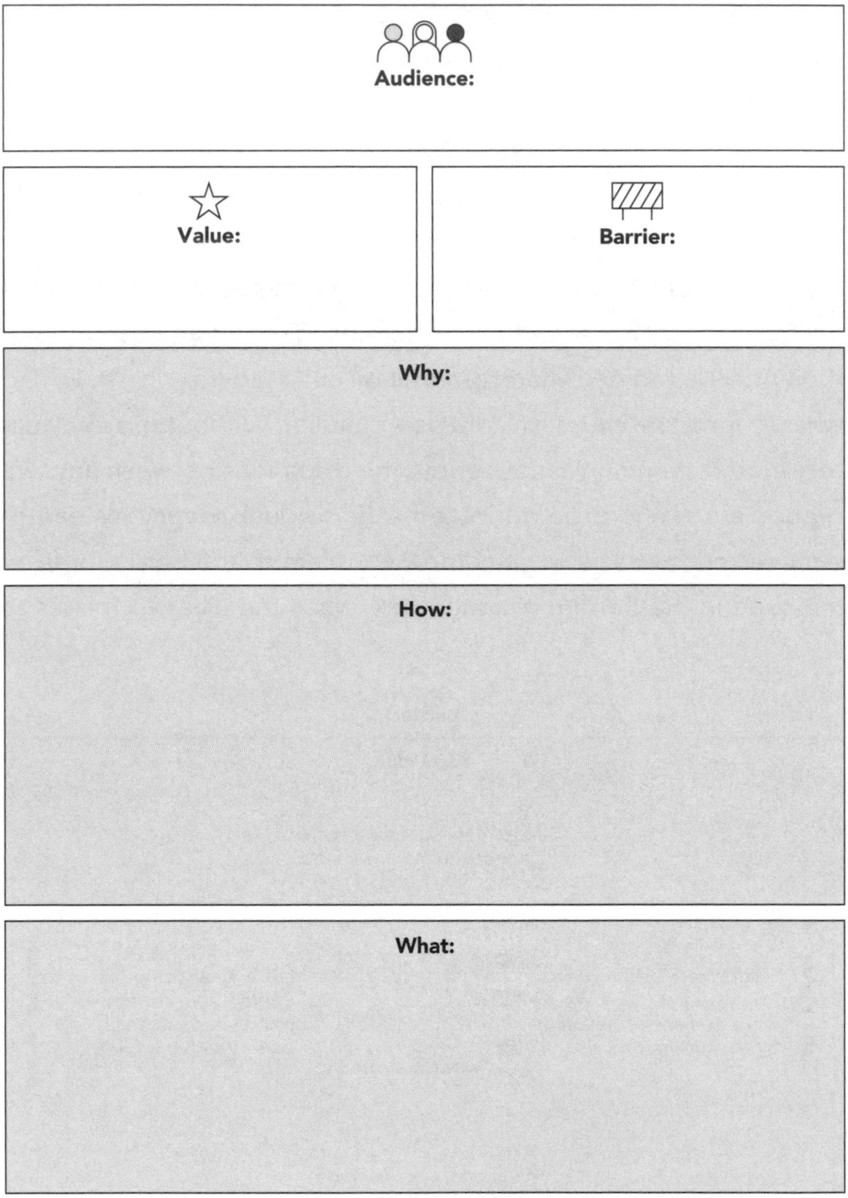

Figure 8. Brevity & Wit's message template.

the ask, and together they form a causal link that allows the messenger to help the audience see the system.

Let's look at this message template in action. In 2019, Brevity & Wit helped the Horizon Foundation, which seeks to improve health in Howard County, Maryland, design a message frame and report to get elected leaders to address systemic racial health disparities. We began by identifying our target audience: elected officials, local policy makers, and community leaders—a group of power brokers who have the power to redesign the system. Sabine then interviewed a representative sample from this group about their values and mindsets. Her research enabled us to identify barriers to our goal and assess the community's level of understanding of systemic racism in health care and well-being.

In collaboration with our partners at Horizon, we decided to tap into the shared value among Howard County residents of wanting to "be the best." The county had a history of ranking at the top of indices of health, education, and quality of life in Maryland, and many residents were invested in maintaining that status. Horizon Foundation officials identified what they wanted their target audience to do: commit to taking a systemic perspective when developing solutions to address health disparities in the county. We identified the greatest barrier to this ask: individualism, or not seeing the system. Explaining the why and how allowed us to break through this barrier by unifying Howard County leaders around their shared goal and inviting them to understand how the system works. Nested under the how is the option to incorporate data or explanations that facilitate understanding. We then crafted the initial message shown in figure 9.

Audience:
Elected officials, policy makers, community leaders

Value:
Being the best (the best county, doing the best for the next generation)

Barrier:
Individualism; not seeing the system

Why:
We all want Howard County to be the best, a 21st-century county.

How:
The challenges we face in the 21st century and a new decade will require collaboration and cooperation to solve.

By addressing health disparities, we can create a thriving community where every resident can contribute to our county's prosperity and well-being.

What:
By committing to a systems perspective and examining root causes, elected officials, community leaders, and residents can create solutions that work for all of us and a more sustainable future for our children.

Figure 9. Brevity & Wit's initial messaging for Horizon Foundation.

Next, we took this message to Horizon's grantees—the organizations that would be affected if the target audience applied a systemic lens to racial health disparities. We sought their input first on this prototype message so we could center the needs of those who would be most affected. With their feedback, we developed a lengthier report and sent it to members of our target audience. Here is an excerpt from the introduction:

> For decades, Howard County has been known for its forward-thinking approach to creating the highest quality of life, serving as a national example of how people of diverse backgrounds can create a thriving community.
>
> And yet, while we have experienced much progress and success, the future presents new challenges to our county. Population growth, environmental risks, demographic shifts and economic constraints will test our community in the years to come.
>
> Because of our existing strengths, Howard County is uniquely positioned to address these challenges with determination and innovation. . . . We have the ability to be the healthiest, best county in the nation if we invest in our future now so everyone can thrive in Howard County.
>
> How do we do this?
>
> The Horizon Foundation believes that one of the most important assignments for the next generation of Howard County residents will be eliminating health disparities so that everyone can lead a long, healthy life. . . . Unfortunately, even in our county, your zip code, skin color, income and other demographic factors can determine your health in very unfair ways.

What's driving these differences?

A system of policies, practices and programs that were not designed to serve everyone equally.

When it comes to inequity, we must recognize a difficult truth: From the nation's founding to today, our society has been designed to benefit some more than others. While a number of past injustices have been addressed by public policy, their legacies persist, and new injustices have emerged. Still, Howard County has emerged from this history well-positioned to address the unequal access to opportunities and outcomes that remains in our community. We are people who value community, innovation, hard work, education and ensuring fair and just opportunities to build a successful future.

Our history of cooperation and collaboration inspires us now more than ever to innovate and create the best future as the nation's leading county where *everyone* can be healthy and prosper.[8]

As you can see, we first unite the audience around this shared value and present the threat to it (inequity). We then explain why this threat was happening; the report later explains racial disparities in health in greater detail. We placed the ask at the end of the report, which enabled us to present more data before the conclusion so we could break through the barrier of rugged individualism.

This process and our message template can be used in both internal and external communications, and you can, and should, tailor it for different groups in your organization. If you're promoting salary transparency to advance equity in your company, your financial department may need to know the return on investment of salary transparency, while your communications team may need to know how it affects brand perception and marketing. Be specific about the returns for your investment in IDEA. If you're not, prepare for pushback.

Guidance for Nonpartisan Institutions

IDEA work is inherently apolitical. However, some ideas have become politicized, and nonpartisan organizations may have difficulty finding their footing in this work. If your organization is nonpartisan, follow these guiding principles to frame IDEA work:

- IDEA work is about bridging across difference. The D is for diversity, which means people get to be different.
- Differences are tolerated so long as they don't dehumanize people. Dehumanization is the process of making a person or group seem less than human and thereby not worthy of humane treatment. No organization should tolerate dehumanization.

When your external communications rely on your reputation of nonpartisanship, frame your commitment to IDEA as part of your commitment to democracy. As we'll explore in the concluding chapter, *democracy* and *capitalism* are not synonymous. In recent years, politicians on the right and left of the ideological spectrum have routinely sought to preserve capitalist structures while eroding democratic ones. Nonpartisan organizations can stand against dehumanization without endorsing a political party by distinguishing democracy from capitalism.

In validating nonpartisanship, I am not advocating for neutrality. In the immortal words of Elie Wiesel, author and Holocaust survivor, "Neutrality helps the oppressor."[9] If your nonpartisan organization is committed to IDEA, you must stand against dehumanization and fascism, ideologies that have sadly become political platforms. You should also be pragmatic enough to prepare a crisis communications plan to respond to the possible backlash you may experience. Remember, IDEA requires courage. Change is always hard, always upsets some people, and always involves loss. But it also involves gain. And the future gain of equal access to opportunity for all is worth the difficult work we need to do today. Nonpartisan organizations play an important role in bridging the divides in our society, but they can't do so without courage and commitment.

Creating Equity through Media and Marketing

If bias is the thumbprint of culture on the brain, then media are the inkpad. With the advent of social media, any organization with a digital presence is part of the media ecosystem. Media are more than news and entertainment programs; they're all the content we consume, from marketing and advertising to PR stunts and blog posts. And media are *exceptionally* powerful. As media scholar Christopher Bell explains in his 2015 TEDx talk,

> In media studies, we spend a lot of time saying that media can't tell us what to think, and they can't; they're terrible at that. But that's not their job. Media don't tell us what to think. Media tell us what to think *about*. They control the conversation, and in controlling the conversation, they don't have to get you to think what they want you to think. They'll just get you thinking about the things they want you to think about, and more importantly, not thinking about things they don't want you to think about. They control the conversation. (Emphasis added.)[1]

In controlling the conversation, media also show us how to behave. Numerous studies by psychologist Albert Bandura and others have shown that people, particularly children, model their behavior off of what they see.[2] This human phenomenon, called social learning theory, is the basis of the work created by Sesame Workshop, the creator of *Sesame Street* and its international coproductions. Many years ago, I worked as an educational content specialist in Sesame Workshop's international education, research, and outreach department and saw firsthand the power of media to shape behavior all over the world. Its international coproductions promoted public health measures like handwashing, taught children how to handle difficult emotions like grief, and, in some countries, even destigmatized playing with children with HIV/AIDS.

But this power to influence is not limited to children's media. As a content creator, you may inadvertently include subtle acts of exclusion (to use DEI consultant and author Tiffany Jana's phrase) in the media you help shape. These small decisions may normalize bias and othering and, eventually, dehumanization and oppression. Making matters worse, marketing "best practices" often leverage cognitive biases to achieve marketing goals. Accent bias, for example, makes us trust people who sound like we do over those who sound different. The scientific explanation is that it is less taxing on the brain to understand someone who has the same accent. But the brain then comes to the false conclusion that ease of understanding is equivalent to truth.[3] We are more likely to believe people who sound like us because they are easier to understand, not because what they say is truer. But when marketers leverage accent bias to sell products, they encode a cultural bias about who is a trusted authority and who is not.

Savvy and equitable marketers are highly attuned to the cultural and cognitive biases of their target market—and subvert them. My company name offers an example. I knew I could not use my own name because, for many people, Minal Bopaiah is difficult to pronounce and spell and, therefore, difficult to remember. Calling my company Bopaiah Consulting would have made it much harder for me to remain "top of mind" or generate word-of-mouth marketing, which is the most valuable marketing channel. Brevity & Wit is memorable—so memorable, in fact, that clients learn how to spell and pronounce *my* name correctly.

Media have the power to mitigate bias and promote equity on a systemic level. To help with that effort, NonprofitAF.com writer and speaker Vu Le (pronounced "Voo Lay") created the REACH equity content screen, which Le allowed me to share. (The full screen, with some of my additions to Le's version, is available at the end of this chapter and at www.TheEquityBook.com.) REACH stands for representation, experience, accessibility, compensation, and harm reduction. Let's dive into why each principle is important for content creation that advances equity.

Representation

In 2016, Perla Nation, then a college student at the University of California, Berkeley, shared a story on Tumblr about taking her Mexican father to see *Rogue One*, the Star Wars spin-off movie starring Diego Luna. In the viral post, she wrote,

> I took my father to see Rogue One today. I've wanted to take him for a while. I wanted my Mexican father, with his thick Mexican accent, to experience what it was like to see a *hero*

in a blockbuster film, speak the way he does. And although I wasn't sure if it was going to resonate with him, I took him anyway. When Diego Luna's character came on screen and started speaking, my dad nudged me and said, "he has a heavy accent." I was like, "Yup." When the film was over and we were walking to the car, he turns to me and says, "did you notice that he had an accent?" And I said, "Yeah, dad, just like yours." Then my dad asked me if the film had made a lot of money. I told him it was the second highest grossing film of 2016 despite it only being out for 18 days in 2016 (since new year just came around). He then asked me if people liked the film, I told him that it had a huge following online and great reviews. He then asked me why Diego Luna hadn't changed his accent and I told him that Diego has openly talked about keeping his accent and how proud he is of it. And my dad was silent for a while and then he said, "And he was a main character." And I said, "He was." And my dad was so happy. As we drove home he started telling me about other Mexican actors that he thinks should be in movies in America. Representation matters.[4]

Representation really does matter in media. And while we have made strides, we have a long way to go. The Geena Davis Institute on Gender in Media, founded by actor Geena Davis, conducts research on media representation of six identities: gender, race, LGBTQ+, disability, age, and body size. In 2019, lead female characters in major films reached parity with male leads for the first time ever. Nearly half (48 percent) of leads in the top one hundred grossing family films were female, double the number in 2007, according to the institute. However, less than 33 percent of leads were women of color. And, while the percentage of lead characters of color rose dramatically over the last decade, White characters were more likely to be portrayed as upper class and as leaders.[5]

In a separate report, the institute found that male characters, though overrepresented, are conscribed to a very narrow definition of masculinity in many films. "Media reinforces the idea that 'real men' are self-sufficient, tough, physically attractive without effort, engage in high-risk behaviors, and value paid labor but not care-giving," the report states.[6] This stereotype harms boys and men because it forces them to live in a constrained space. Most nota-bly, male characters were less likely than female characters to show emotions, including empathy, happiness, and even anger. Given the importance of empathy and emotional intelligence in designing for equity, it's no wonder we're still struggling to design systems that are fair and just!

Content creators can counter these trends and their harmful impact on society by allowing male characters to express a full range of emotions. Let them model close friendships, family relationships, and healthy expressions of emotions. Show boys and young men asking for help, particularly from their parents. Avoid depicting boys and men as solitary or as having to go it alone, which triggers the rugged individualist bias.

Representation of difference is also important when selecting visuals for marketing materials, including social media and web-site images, especially if a brand is seeking to attract audiences of diverse backgrounds. The solution to underrepresentation is not **tokenism**—the practice of making only a perfunctory or sym-bolic effort to include people from marginalized groups to give the appearance of equity. I've observed that people from margin-alized groups can detect tokenism long before people with more centered identities. If you are White, for example, and seeking more racial diversity at your organization, or if you are nondisabled and seeking more representation of disability, then you are likely not a good judge of tokenism. You need people of those various identities to question your efforts and weigh in.

Another challenge to increasing representation in visual imagery is the bias encoded in the search algorithms of many stock image databases. When I type "attractive woman" into Shutterstock, the first page of results is predominantly images of White women. Only a few are of Black and Asian women. All appear to be able-bodied, and all are a similar size and shape. Still, this is progress; two years ago, every image on the first page of results was of a White woman.

But even images of various races and genders can subtly support White supremacy and patriarchal ideas. My friend Acacia Betancourt runs the Instagram account @SpottingRacism, and she shows how numerous images—from public health posters to product packaging—promote White supremacy by assuming White people are the default. Even in images of multiracial groups, White people are often centered and foregrounded, while darker-skinned people are on the periphery or in the background.

Instead of tokenism, include people of different genders, races, abilities, body sizes, and sexualities in thoughtful ways. Start by involving individuals with those backgrounds in the creative process. Also, consider using stock photo databases that counter cultural biases. Visit www.TheEquityBook.com for an updated list.

Finally, keep **intersectionality** in mind during photo selection, especially when it comes to certain dimensions of diversity. Photos representing disability rights are often whitewashed, in that they include only White people with disabilities. These images are also often of people who are cisgender and straight. Disability rights is an intersectional movement, and we need images of people with disabilities that represent the full spectrum of humanity.

Experience

When it comes to content creation, we must all have the humility to ask ourselves, "Am I the appropriate person to talk about this issue, and is my organization the most appropriate one to address it?" Do you have lived experience or expertise in the subject? If not, are there people whose work you should credit, even if it hasn't been published? And when you do invest the time to learn about other cultures, are you at risk of culture appropriation?

According to the website Everyday Feminism, cultural appropriation is a specific "power dynamic in which members of a dominant culture take elements from a culture of people who have been systematically oppressed by that dominant group."[7] It's different from cultural exchange, where people share mutually with one another. But it can be tricky to know which is which; wise marketing and communications professionals err on the side of caution.

One television show that has handled cultural exchange and representation well is *Molly of Denali*, a PBS Kids cartoon featuring Molly Mabray, the first Alaskan Native protagonist in a children's show. The creators, which included Atomic Cartoons and WGBH Kids, didn't simply drop an Alaskan Native character into standard plotlines. Instead, they hired and worked with Indigenous creators in all aspects of the production, both on-screen and behind the scenes. Every Indigenous character is voiced by an Indigenous actor, and the theme song is sung by Indigenous performers using Indigenous instruments.

The show's marketing is also respectful and inclusive. For Halloween, the show released a graphic on social media encouraging fans to wear a brown coat, boots, blue jeans, and pink mittens, as Molly does in almost every episode, but forgo dressing in her Native attire. "Molly's traditional Native dress is an important part of her culture and should not be worn as a costume," the image states.[8]

Accessibility

Accessibility is about ensuring that anyone who wants to enjoy your content can. More than 56 million Americans (or 19 percent of the population) have a disability.[9] Designing content all people can use is a moral imperative. It also makes good financial sense: people with disabilities have $175 billion in discretionary spending power, according to the US Department of Justice.[10] They should command the respect of marketers and content creators.

While accessibility is an expansive topic, thinking about the following five dimensions of ability is a good place to start if you want to increase your content's accessibility and appeal:

- Vision
- Hearing
- Mobility
- Cognitive ability
- Culture

Please note that a person's ability in any dimension may not be a permanent state. People may suffer from situational blindness, as when they are driving and can't look at their phone (for which GPS voice narration is helpful). Or they may experience temporary deafness if they have an ear infection (for which closed captioning is helpful). Some of today's most beloved innovations were created when others considered dimensions of disability and designed accordingly. In the words of Elise Roy, Salesforce's vice president of product accessibility and inclusive design, "Disability drives innovation."[11]

Vision

At Brevity & Wit, we usually begin the progression toward greater accessibility by encouraging strong color contrast in all visual designs. Yellow text on a white background, for example, is difficult for people with low vision to see. When creating a logo, we ensure that it meets the standards set forth by the Web Content Accessibility Guidelines (WCAG) 2.0, the gold standard in web accessibility. And WebAIM (www.WebAIM.org), an organization that supports online accessibility, has a color contrast checker that allows people to see if logo colors meet those standards. It also offers services to identify design elements that may interfere with accessibility, like type size and page hierarchy.

We also encourage using alt text whenever possible. Many blind and vision-impaired people navigate digital content via screen readers, which use alt text—a layer of metadata invisible to sighted users—to describe images, buttons, and graphics.[12] Including thoughtful alt text when designing websites, email newsletters, and digital documents allows screen readers to "read" images to people with poor vision.

In September 2020, when I interviewed Kim Locraft, design director at Forum One, a web design agency, she cautioned that content may comply with web accessibility guidelines but still be useless. For example, including alt text that says "shirt" is better than no alt text at all for a visually impaired user, but it is of little help when the user is shopping for a shirt online. Be thoughtful in your use of alt text or hire someone who is.

Hearing

Including captions and subtitles in your videos and audio files can do a lot for people with hearing impairments. This is especially true for streaming content, like TV shows, webinars, presentations, and even video conferences.

The National Endowment for the Arts created a handy list of tips and resources to increase accessibility to virtual events that became necessary after the emergence of COVID-19.[13] Resources and tips include the following:

- Use presentation software that allows live captioning, like Google Slides or PowerPoint.
- Leave the bottom of presentation slides blank so captions don't cover content.
- Consider hiring a sign language interpreter. The Registry of Interpreters for the Deaf, Inc., offers a list of professionals.[14]
- Use videoconferencing software that allows captioning, such as Zoom and BlueJeans.
- Use video-sharing services like YouTube that will caption uploaded videos.

Mobility

Designing online content to accommodate mobility challenges requires making content and interaction accessible via keyboard alone. For example, how do you design content for people who don't use a mouse because they have one hand? The optimal solution is to ensure that all keys can be hit by one finger and that interaction doesn't depend on striking two keys at the same time. This may seem counterintuitive to many web designers, but it is not difficult to do. Some online survey tools already do this.

Another innovation is voice-recognition software, which aids website navigation. This software abounds, though you may not realize it. It's used in airline departure and arrival information systems, banking transactions, automated phone appointment reminders, automated telephone receptionists, and more.

Cognitive Ability

Cognitive diversity includes learning disorders, like dyslexia and attention deficit hyperactivity disorder (ADHD); mood disorders, like anxiety and depression; and cognitive disorders, like Asperger's syndrome and autism spectrum disorder. Unfortunately, there is still a lot of stigma and bias around cognitive diversity, which means it gets little attention or money, whether through funding for treatment or research or even within accessibility budgets. In 2016, I wrote an op-ed in the *Stanford Social Innovation Review* advocating for more attention to mental health and cognitive diversity. In my piece, I asked why we don't use the term "psychosis survivor" as readily as we use the term "cancer survivor."[15] Sadly, I'm still asking this question today. The full expression of equity will need to address these gaps in accessibility for cognitive diversity.

In the meantime, Locraft advises writing at a seventh grade reading level to support comprehension among people of various cognitive abilities, as well as among nonnative English speakers and people who might be multitasking. Equity is recognizing that everyone, regardless of cognitive ability, has a right to access information on the internet.

Culture

Culture isn't normally discussed in conversations about accessible content, but it should be. The Hootsuite's 2020 global digital report estimates that 4.5 billion people use the internet, or 59 percent of the world's population.[16] With that many global users, we need to discuss cross-cultural design and how to make content accessible and appealing to people in other countries. We must also consider how internet use differs by region and country. Of the nearly 8 billion people on this planet, only 1 billion have access to high-speed internet.[17] In some countries, like Vietnam and India, mobile phones are the primary interface for internet use. In others, like Myanmar, internet is synonymous with Facebook.

When designing for equity on the web, you need an idea of how global your reach is so you can tailor content to different cultures within your target audience. Senongo Akpem, author of the book *Cross-Cultural Design*, designed a web page for a climate change nonprofit organization featuring its areas of impact. He incorporated a map of the Northern Hemisphere that was free to use via a Creative Commons license from Wikipedia. But the map did not show disputed territories in India and China, a major area where the organization was working.[18] Akpem eventually changed the map to suit the audience, since boundaries are a big part of national identity. Once again, involving colleagues and audiences from different cultures is critical when designing for a global footprint.

Compensation

Compensation asks, "Who is getting paid for content creation, and is it fair?" Earlier, we shared the example of *Molly of Denali*, which demonstrates how to center a marginalized community—not only by involving community members in content creation but also by paying them for their contributions.

When I lecture to nonprofit fundraisers and marketers, I often say that if they're really committed to equity, they need to pay the beneficiaries they interview for their fundraising and marketing campaign stories. Nonprofit organizations are not news organizations; they raise money from the stories and experiences of others. Equity means paying sources for their stories the way one pays Deloitte consultants for their time. Some may scoff, but nonprofit leaders have successfully implemented equitable policies like these. My friend Sarah Boison was the director of communications from 2019 to 2021 at Communities in Schools, a nonprofit organization that supports students throughout their education. At conferences and in webinars, she often shares how Communities in Schools authentically embodies its commitment to equity and inclusion not only by paying students for their stories but also by giving them decision-making roles in the organization. In fact, President and CEO Rey Saldaña is an alumnus of the Communities in Schools program.

Harm Reduction

IDEA starts with ceasing to do harm. It doesn't matter if you intended to cause harm or not. In a complex system, our actions always have unintended consequences, and equitable leaders aren't afraid to take accountability for them.

In the REACH equity content screen, questions about not causing harm center on many of the biases, stigmas, and stereotypes we've discussed. You should also focus on building equitable relationships over the long term. Brevity & Wit recently worked with leaders of a nonprofit organization seeking more equitable visual imagery. We recommended that they allow those featured in their photographs to revoke the use of their image at a later date. In a digital world where nothing disappears, an equitable policy like this allows people to protect themselves and their privacy should they experience domestic violence or other forms of oppression or violence in the future. We recommended listing a contact email address on all permission forms. Photo subjects should also receive a copy of the signed form for their records. The leaders acknowledged they would need to create a process for tracking photos and permissions moving forward to enact this policy and are in the midst of doing so. This kind of redesigning of existing systems and structures is undoubtedly more work, but it can truly change how people's images are licensed and used, ensuring greater protection and safety for people exposed to violence and oppression.

THE REACH EQUITY CONTENT SCREEN[19]

Representation: How does the issue you're exploring affect people of diverse identities?

- People of color, including Black and Indigenous folks
- Women
- Immigrants/refugees
- People with disabilities, visible and invisible
- LGBTQ+ folks
- Transgender and intersex individuals
- People of different income levels
- Older adults
- Youth and younger folks
- People of different religions
- Parents of young children, caregivers
- Neurodiverse individuals
- Rural communities
- People of varying levels of formal education

Experience: Are you the appropriate person/organization to be talking about this issue?

- Do you need, and have, the lived experience to talk about this issue?
- Are there people from the above list who have written/ spoken about this issue that you should give credit to?
- Are you appropriating from other cultures in creating this content?
- Are you Columbusing ("discovering" something that was already in existence)?

Accessibility: Can everyone access your content?

- Are there descriptions/alt text on every image?
- Are there captions/subtitles on your videos?
- Is there sufficient contrast in terms of text and background?
- Are font sizes big enough?
- Are your links underlined instead of just a different color, which may not be helpful to color-blind people?
- If you're doing a video or podcast, did you provide a complete transcript?
- Is your language too academic or full of jargon?
- Are your acronyms spelled out?
- Can people from different countries access your content?

Compensation: Who is getting paid; is it equitable?

- Are you, or will you be, benefiting financially or in other ways from this content?
- If you are getting compensated, does it make sense for you to be compensated? (For instance, if you're not Native, should you get paid for an article about Native issues?)

- Are you compensating people equitably to help create and distribute this content?
- Are you using women- and minority-owned businesses?

Harm reduction: Is your content unintentionally causing harm?

- Are the examples you use reinforcing stereotypes? (For instance, if you mention a fictional doctor or engineer to illustrate a point, did you make that person male?)
- Is the language you use reinforcing gender binaries, such as using "he or she" when you could just use "they"?
- Are you making vast generalizations about whole groups of people? For instance, millennials or boomers?
- Are you shaming people of different body types?
- Are you reinforcing stigma against poor people, such as calling something "low-class"?
- Are you casually using words like "tribe" and "spirit animal" that may have significant meaning to Native and other communities?
- Are you making light of medical conditions such as alcoholism?
- Are you using words that are ableist, like "tone-deaf"?
- Are you using language that further stigmatizes mental health, such as "that meeting was crazy"?
- Are you using unethical patterns or other duplicitous methods to benefit your organization's revenues over people?

Bear in mind that equity cannot be achieved in just one piece of content; equity is a long-term effort that must be assessed over a body of work. Equitable leaders are aware of how their media presence either reinforces or subverts stereotypes. They also make sure that all content is inclusive, accessible, and respectful to all populations. Most importantly, equitable leaders know that ethical media creators do not ignore the findings of social science. As we've discussed, social science has long documented the psychological and societal impact of the media. Equitable content creators harness those findings to cocreate a more equitable world.

Cocreating an Equitable World

May there be such a oneness between us that when one
weeps the other tastes salt.

—Kahlil Gibran

In June 2019, five hundred Wayfair employees walked out of the company headquarters in Boston to protest the sale of beds to US Immigration and Customs Enforcement (ICE) detention centers where children and parents seeking refuge were being separated and locked in cages.[1]

In March 2020, dozens of employees at the publishing company Hachette walked out of its company headquarters in New York City to protest the company's decision to publish a memoir by alleged child molester Woody Allen.[2]

Later in 2020, in the middle of the pandemic, hundreds of Facebook employees staged a virtual walkout by taking the day off to protest their leadership's decision to allow Donald Trump to post false, inflammatory, and racist posts.[3]

As more and more individuals begin to recognize the reality of interdependence and organize for big changes, their power grows. And leaders will be forced to respond.

For companies looking to recruit and retain top talent in the twenty-first century, corporate social responsibility, social impact, or whatever other name it goes by is no longer a nice-to-have; it's a must-have. "Younger employees and customers have come to see practices such as sustainability and community economic empowerment as mandatory for their loyalty," writes Rohini Anand, a business leader who served as global chief diversity officer at Sodexo.[4] In short, whether leaders choose to cocreate a more equitable world or not will directly impact their ability to hire talent, woo customers, and ensure profitability in the twenty-first century.

However, if we only do good so we can bask in the glow of a beloved brand or higher profits, we are setting our moral compass according to the opinions of others. If or when opinions change, we will lose our bearings. That's not to say we should ignore evolving opinions about *how* to do good. But consumers and employees seek authenticity in the brands with which they interact, and they hold organizations accountable for **virtue signaling**.[5] Equally detrimental is falling prey to the "shiny new object" syndrome. Leaders and staff who are attracted to and seduced by the next trending social cause fail to commit time and money to sustainable change. They end up sticking their fingers in the proverbial dam instead of seriously confronting and addressing the enormous threats to equity we face, from environmental degradation to racial injustice to a possible pandemic far more deadly than COVID-19.

Both individuals and organizations can respond to the call for social justice in our society in many ways, regardless of rank (but with an awareness of their power).

Individual Power for Change

Everyone, regardless of their position in an organization, can begin to cocreate a more equitable world by joining a cause or movement that is intersectional. This requires some amount of research; historically, many mission-based organizations have not been intersectional because they saw their job as advocating for *their* issue, even if that meant complementary causes got less money or attention. In recent years, organizations like Planned Parenthood and the Sierra Club have begun to examine their founders' racist ideologies and take concrete steps to eradicate the legacy of such thinking in their work and workplace.

Secondly, individuals should find productive ways to pressure their workplaces to advance equity. This needn't always result in a walkout (though it might if the organization's leaders are not particularly inclusive or humble enough to listen). To be effective, employees should focus on marrying calls for change with the organization's interests. In the examples from Wayfair, Hachette, and Facebook, the employees' expectations were reasonable given their employers' power and scope of operations. But I once heard about a director of fundraising who did not want to run any fundraising campaigns in nonprofit media after the murder of George Floyd because she felt that every cent people had to give should go toward Black Lives Matter. While I understand the sentiment, one needs a long-term lens; a loss of funding threatens job security for all employees, and Black and Brown people were more likely to lose their jobs during the COVID-19 pandemic. Insolvency does not advance equity. Thus, employees—regardless of rank—need to develop a systems lens and learn to bridge across difference when calling for leadership to advance equity in the wider world.

As you climb an organization's hierarchical ladder, you can use your incremental gains in power to advance equity even if your superiors are not yet fully on board. You can begin to cocreate a more equitable world by organizing with your counterparts at peer organizations or through industry associations. Recently, the Communications Network, an organization of foundation and nonprofit communications professionals, released a report benchmarking racial equity communications in the sector.[6] The report's accompanying website has data, tools, and case studies to educate communicators on how they can use their sphere of influence to cocreate a more equitable world.[7] Trade associations in finance, marketing, product development, research, and other business functions should look to engage in similar research and education initiatives for their members. This will allow midlevel leaders to use their power to nudge their organizations toward greater equity.

And of course, we cannot underestimate the power of communications, in cocreating an equitable world. Storytelling, like we saw Jack and Bob do in chapter 3, can unmask the system for peers and the public. While the majority of Americans (including myself) felt that pressure, not genuine concern, drove the plethora of public statements denouncing racism in the wake of George Floyd's murder, the Pew Research Center found that most Black (75 percent), Asian (70 percent), and Hispanic (66 percent) adults said that it was at least somewhat important that companies and organizations release statements about political or social issues.[8] In other words, public statements were important to those who have been historically marginalized, even if peer pressure and public perception were the catalysts. What we say matters, even if publicly denouncing inequity is just the first step in creating a more equitable world.

Organizational Power for Change

There is power in organizing. Just as one employee cannot make an organization equitable on their own, one company cannot make the world equitable. And so, a movement among the most senior leaders in organizations across industries and sectors is also needed if we really want to create a more equitable world. In 2017, more than 1,500 CEOs signed the CEO Action for Diversity & Inclusion pledge, making a public commitment to advance diversity and inclusion within the workplace. Signatories commit to enacting four main commitments, and companies that have already enacted some of them serve as mentors for other companies.[9]

This is a good first step, but more is needed. If we want to cocreate a more equitable world, senior leaders at corporations, nonprofits, public institutions, and government bodies need to organize a cross-sector movement committed to one unifying idea: defend democracy.

Many people, from academics to media pundits to average citizens, treat capitalism and democracy as if they are synonyms. But, as Harvard professor Rebecca Henderson demonstrates in her seminal article on the subject, they are not.[10] In the *Harvard Business Review*, she argues that countries like Russia, China, and Turkey prove that capitalism without democracy is possible. And in fact, the Economist Intelligence Unit's Democracy Index downgraded the United States to a "flawed democracy" in 2019.[11]

In the past fifty years, corporations have bought political influence to cut taxes, block and eliminate federal regulation of industry, reduce funding for public education and social welfare initiatives, weaken public and private labor unions, restrict voter registration, and cut back voting days and hours. They fought against the policies and structures implemented by the New Deal, while benefiting from the roads and infrastructure it built, and against social support programs like Medicare and the Affordable Care Act, from which they also benefit by having access to a healthy workforce. They have clashed with the free press and flooded the political system with tainted money to control policy (belying their antiregulatory spin; in fact, they *support* regulation, so long as it benefits business).[12]

As Henderson explains, the result is not a triumphant free market. Instead of a healthy democracy and free market, our system favors the rich and the well-connected at the expense of the rest of us. Income inequality is disturbingly high, and the planet is literally on fire as I write this, with wildfires turning California's fabled blue sky a dusty orange. Without a functioning democracy, extremism abounds, both on the left and the right.[13]

The Pillars of Democracy

If businesses *really* want to protect democracy and capitalism, they should advocate for Henderson's four pillars of a thriving free market:[14]

1. An impartial justice system
2. Prices that reflect true costs
3. Real competition
4. Freedom of opportunity

We need an impartial justice system to uphold legal and social contracts; indeed, free market capitalism depends on market actors keeping their promises, and a corrupt justice system cannot ensure that. Similarly, we need prices for goods and services that reflect true costs so that corporations can achieve profitability and sustainability without government subsidies. Accurate pricing would consider the effect of the production of goods on our environment and incorporate the cost of health care for workers. In our country, the cost of coal and corn is artificially low, thanks to government subsidies of these industries. And too many corporations use the legal loophole of "contract" work to deny health care to talented, reliable individuals working full time. These practices have contributed to an unhealthy environment and an unhealthy workforce, which only hurts employers in the end anyway.

We need real competition to foster innovation and efficiency in a free market. But real competition requires regulations that safeguard fair play. Markets are genuinely free only when everyone can participate. This fosters freedom of opportunity. As I explained earlier, my marriage made it possible for me to start my company; I couldn't do it as a single person because I needed affordable health insurance and a financial buffer to get started. Without the public structures that support freedom of opportunity, like quality public education and universal health care, only the rich and powerful (or the married and dual-incomed) can start businesses, meaning society loses out on the talent and innovation of millions of people.

To cocreate equity in the world, business leaders must question their assumptions and biases about the marriage of democracy and capitalism—and see capitalism as democracy's servant. This is an ironic metaphor, I know, for a book about equity. But capitalism can clearly survive, and even thrive, without democracy. If we want democracy to survive, we cannot allow capitalism to suck its lifeblood for bigger and bigger profits. Our money must serve our values.

The Role of Nonprofits

Lest my friends in the nonprofit sector think they are off the hook, I must note that many nonprofit organizations perpetuate systems of inequity, both within their organizations and in their fields. Having worked in nonprofit organizations for a good portion of my career, I have seen it all: discriminatory hiring practices, race-based gaslighting, overt sexual harassment, and more. Most troubling is the sector's willingness to collude with the hoarding of wealth by the few.

If the nonprofit sector is committed to cocreating equity in the world, it needs to take a hard look at its fundraising mechanisms. Edgar Villanueva, author of *Decolonizing Wealth: Indigenous Wisdom to Heal Divides and Restore Balance*, writes that the way forward in philanthropy is through reparations. "The spirit of reparations is that those who hold the bulk of ill-gotten resources and influence must hold responsibility for repairing the harms done. As movers of money, [foundations and philanthropists] have the ability to take immediate action to get resources into the hands of those who have been marginalized and excluded by wealth-holding institutions for generations."[15] Collectively, US foundations have roughly $1 trillion in assets. (For context, the United States government allocated $934 billion for defense in 2020–21 and $41 billion for foreign assistance.)[16] Villanueva recommends that foundations begin tithing 10 percent of their assets and establish a trust fund led by Native and Black Americans to support asset-building projects, such as home ownership, education, and business startup funds.[17]

In my talks with leaders of foundations and nonprofit organizations, I have floated the radically equitable idea of persuading philanthropists to advocate for higher taxes for high earners like themselves. That is the single most powerful thing they can do to build a more just society. Billionaire philanthropist Warren Buffett, in fact, regularly advocates for this. Paying more taxes would not only redistribute ill-gotten wealth but would also allow such wealth to be distributed through a democratic process.

It is neither equitable nor democratic that so many global health nonprofit organizations must kiss the ring of the Bill and Melinda Gates Foundation (BMGF) to acquire the vast sums of money needed to address systemic problems. What's more, these programs are subject to the approval and consent of BMGF, which is not representative of the people it claims to serve. Large foundations frequently court dictators and tyrants in developing nations in exchange for access and the privilege to operate with little regulation, which further erodes democracy. To wit, BMGF awarded Indian prime minister Narendra Modi its Global Goalkeeper Award for his support of sanitation projects throughout the country—even as he was actively suppressing India's marginalized Dalit and Muslim communities and conducting a communications blackout in the disputed area of Kashmir by cutting off mobile and internet service.[18]

Nonprofit leaders must acknowledge that their work is neither automatically democratic nor equitable; in fact, it is sometimes the opposite. They must begin to value inclusive and equitable processes as much as impact, and they must stop the charade that strategic objectives for social change are similar to corporate objectives or that MBAs and McKinsey consultants naturally make great nonprofit leaders. Not everything is a business, nor should everything be run as one.[19] Some of the most important things in life— our health, our education, caring for others—require significant investments of time, energy, and money. They may be expenses in the short term, but they provide enormous benefits to our interdependent society in the long term.

Closing Thoughts

Equity is a big ask. It requires us to examine our fundamental assumptions about the world. It requires us to think hard about the role of systems and structures in our lives, our communities, and our society and to find a way to make the invisible visible. Mostly, it requires us to dig deep into our internal desire for fairness and summon the courage to do hard things, like redesign entire organizations.

But equity gives more than it takes. When we meet it with bravery and humility, equity gives us innovation and opportunity; it helps us make everyone's life a little bit better. It can save babies in India, allow girls and boys to see themselves as they never have through media, enable people with disabilities to access the informational power of the internet, help launch new businesses, and ensure that no one's life is determined by their differences.

My hope is that this book has opened a door in your mind—a new way of seeing how we can design our organizations and why equity is so critical to IDEA, innovation, and the future of work. In showing you this possibility, I also hope you leave with some concrete tools you can use to start designing for more equity in the corner of the world where you have influence and power. If we all simply did that, we would become drops in a tsunami of justice.

Remember, everything in the human-made world was designed or invented by someone no greater than you. From words to companies, we all make life up as one collective, choose-your-own-adventure tale. We are all designers of our shared destiny. No one among us, no matter how marginalized, is unable to make a difference in the lives of the rest of us. We may not see the effects right away. But we all have the power to create a more just and equitable world because creativity is our birthright as humans.

When we create more equity and justice, we fulfill a very deep human need. So don't delay. Start designing a more equitable world today, however big or small your efforts may be. It is the only way to know the depths of your true humanity.

Discussion Guide

I hope that reading *Equity: How to Design Organizations Where Everyone Thrives* has provided you with new insights about how you can use your power to create a more equitable system for us all. If you are looking to dive deeper into the subject, I have provided some discussion questions and prompts for individuals, teams, and organizations. You can also download these questions and supporting materials at www.TheEquityBook.com.

Individuals

1. What is your family's origin story? If you are Indigenous, how has settler colonialism affected your ancestors and you? If you are the descendent of immigrants, how did your ancestors come to this country?
2. Download the Group Identity Wheel from www.TheEquity Book.com and fill it out. How have you been supported by the system? How have you been marginalized?
3. Think of a recent accomplishment. What factors, other than your own individual effort, contributed to your success?
4. How do the systems you are in stunt your growth or health? What would a supportive system look like?
5. What is your relationship to difference?
6. What does empathy mean to you?

7. Do you usually engage in perspective-taking or perspective-gathering? How can you begin to practice perspective-gathering?

8. What culture or subculture outside of your own are you curious to learn more about? How can you learn more about that culture in a respectful way?

9. How representative is the media you consume of the diversity of your country or community? What other media options can you consume to get a wider perspective?

Teams

1. What are your team norms or "culture"? Think about how you are conditioned to approach deadlines, risk-taking, truth-telling, and conflict management.

2. To what extent are you, as members of a team, comfortable with difference?

3. Name some examples of when teammates were able to accept, leverage, or adapt to difference on a project. Was it helpful?

4. How often do you ask for one another's perspectives?

5. Look at Julie Diamond's seven traits of inclusive leadership at the end of chapter 2. Which ones do you and your team members exhibit most when collaborating?

6. What does equity mean to each of you?

7. What steps can you take as a team to create a more equitable experience for everyone?

Organizations

1. In what ways is your organization equitable? In what ways is it inequitable?
2. Are leaders engaged in IDEA and interested in fostering equity?
3. What groups are historically marginalized or underrepresented in your organization?
4. If you were to center those people, how might you redesign your organization to best suit their needs and lived experiences?
5. How can the organization regularly engage in perspective-gathering to understand employee needs or the barriers that may prevent employees from contributing their strengths to the organization?
6. Are some groups underrepresented in leadership? If so, why do you think they are?
7. If you were to set equitable outcomes for your organization, what would they be?
8. What observable behaviors would get you closer to those outcomes in the next twelve months?
9. Visit www.TheEquityBook.com and watch the YouTube video about *Switch*. What obstacles inhibit the observable behaviors you'd like to see in your organization?
10. What statements has your organization made about IDEA? Do they adhere to the lessons in chapter 5?
11. How inclusive and equitable is your marketing and social media presence? How could it be more inclusive and equitable?
12. Does your organization defend democracy and take a clear stand against dehumanization? If not, why? What would it take for your organization to publicly advocate for democracy and against dehumanization?

Notes

Introduction

1. "The Immigration Act of 1924 (The Johnson-Reed Act)," Office of the Historian, US Department of State, accessed July 18, 2020, https://history.state.gov/milestones/1921-1936/immigration-act.

2. Bruce J. Biddle and David C. Berliner, "A Research Synthesis: Unequal School Funding in the United States," *Educational Leadership* 59, no. 8 (2002): 48–59.

3. Antionette Carroll, "Designing for a More Equitable World," filmed January 2018 in Vancouver, TED video, 5:17, https://www.youtube.com/watch?v=z9XKBgdOrHU.

4. "Antionette Carroll," TED, accessed January 10, 2021, https://www.ted.com/profiles/9072089/about.

5. Isabel Wilkerson, *Caste: The Origins of Our Discontents* (New York: Random House, 2020), 78–88.

6. I am grateful to the Robert Wood Johnson Foundation, which has allowed this image to be reproduced with attribution.

7. Julie O'Mara and Alan Richter, *Global Diversity & Inclusion Benchmarks: Standards for Organizations around the World* (Las Vegas: Centre for Global Inclusion, 2017), https://centreforglobalinclusion.org/wp-content/uploads/2017/09/GDIB-V.090517.pdf.

8. *Merriam-Webster*, s.v. "equity," accessed November 29, 2020, https://www.merriam-webster.com/dictionary/equity.

9. For more information, see https://www.inclusionnextwork.org/.

Chapter 1

1. Mahzarin Banaji, "Can You Change Implicit Bias?" May 25, 2018, *Washington Post*, https://www.washingtonpost.com/video /national/can-you-change-implicit-bias/2018/05/29/e1d28542 -604d-11e8-b656-236c6214ef01_video.html.

2. "Our Models," Hofstede Insights, accessed November 26, 2020, https://hi.hofstede-insights.com/models.

3. Anne Hathaway, "Human Rights Campaign National Dinner Pt. 3," September 15, 2018, Los Angeles, CA, YouTube video, 56:19, https://www.youtube.com/watch?v=6jmyiCkrXNI.

4. Jared M. Spool, "Great Designs Should Be Experienced and Not Seen," Center Centre UIE, May 14, 2009, https://articles.uie.com /experiencedesign.

5. Lauren Williams, "The Co-Constitutive Nature of Neoliberalism, Design, and Racism," *Design and Culture* 11, no. 3 (2019): 301–21, https://doi.org/10.1080/17547075.2019.1656901.

6. *13th*, directed by Ava DuVernay, released October 7, 2016, Netflix.

7. David Jones Media, "How Can We Win Kimberly Jones Video Full Length David Jones Media Clean Edit #BLM 2020 What Can I Do," June 9, 2020, USA, YouTube video, https://www.youtube.com /watch?v=llci8MVh8J4.

8. "The Problem," Moneythink, accessed September 14, 2020, https://moneythink.org/the-problem/.

9. Williams, "The Co-Constitutive Nature," 301–21.

10. Matthew Desmond, "In Order to Understand the Brutality of American Capitalism, You Have to Start on the Plantation," The 1619 Project, ed. Nikole Hannah-Jones, *New York Times*, August 14, 2019, https://www.nytimes.com/interactive/2019/08/14 /magazine/slavery-capitalism.html.

11. Robin J. Ely and Irene Padavic, "What's Really Holding Women Back?" *Harvard Business Review*, March–April 2020, https:// hbr.org/2020/03/whats-really-holding-women-back.

12. Ely and Padavic.

13. Brené Brown, *Braving the Wilderness: The Quest for True Belonging and the Courage to Stand Alone* (New York: Random House, 2019), 74.

Chapter 2

1. "Design Census 2019," AIGA, accessed November 29, 2020, https://designcensus.org/.
2. Jesse Weaver, "Design Has an Empathy Problem: White Men Can't Design for Everyone," Medium, June 15, 2020, https:// uxdesign.cc/design-has-an-empathy-problem-white-men-cant -design-for-everyone-4eef12f0f2b.
3. Jessica Bennett, "What If Instead of Calling People Out, We Called Them In?" *New York Times*, November 19, 2020, https:// www.nytimes.com/2020/11/19/style/loretta-ross-smith-college -cancel-culture.html.
4. Nicholas Epley, "Be Mindwise: Perspective Taking vs. Perspective Getting," *Behavioral Scientist*, April 16, 2014, https://behavioralscientist .org/be-mindwise-perspective-taking-vs-perspective-getting/.
5. Heather Caruso, "Record Numbers of Americans Recognize Racism as a Problem. What Could the Solution Be Like?" *Behavioral Scientist*, June 29, 2020, https://behavioralscientist.org /record-numbers-of-americans-recognize-racism-as-a-problem -what-could-the-solution-be-like/.
6. Epley, "Be Mindwise."
7. Chip Heath and Dan Heath, *Switch: How to Change Things When Change Is Hard* (New York: Random House, 2011).
8. Lisa Kepinski and Tinna C. Nielsen, *The Inclusion Nudges Guidebook* (self-pub., 2020).
9. Anne Helen Petersen, "Other Countries Have Social Safety Nets. The US Has Women," Culture Study, November 11, 2020, https:// annehelen.substack.com/p/other-countries-have-social-safety.
10. Heath and Heath, *Switch*.

11. Durell Coleman and Marie Trudelle, "How to Make Design Thinking More Disability Inclusive," *Stanford Social Innovation Review,* March 22, 2019, https://ssir.org/articles/entry /how_to_make_design_thinking_more_disability_inclusive.

12. Saige Perry, "Our Top 10 Stories of 2019," IDEO, December 20, 2019, http://www.ideo.com/blog/our-top-10-stories-of-2019.

13. Zameena Mejia, "Steve Jobs: Here's What Most People Get Wrong about Focus," CNBC, October 2, 2018, https://www.cnbc .com/2018/10/02/steve-jobs-heres-what-most-people-get-wrong -about-focus.html.

14. Dacher Keltner, *The Power Paradox: How We Gain and Lose Influence* (New York: Penguin Books, 2017), 3.

15. Cyndi Suarez, *The Power Manual: How to Master Complex Power Dynamics* (Gabriola Island, BC: New Society Publishers, 2018), 13.

16. Suarez, 15.

17. The Winters Group, Inc., "I am seeing some organizations empower their DEI and HR leadership as full interdependent partners . . . ," LinkedIn, September 2020, https://www.linkedin .com/posts/the-winters-group-inc-_diversityandinclusion- inclusionanddiversity-activity-6706343562792980480-Ikrx.

18. Julie Diamond, "The Role of Power in Creating Inclusive Workplaces," Diamond Leadership, accessed October 1, 2020, https://diamondleadership.com/wp-content/uploads/2020/06 /creating-inclusive-organizational-cultures-white-paper.pdf.

Chapter 3

1. Cyndi Suarez, *The Power Manual: How to Master Complex Power Dynamics* (Gabriola Island, BC: New Society Publishers, 2018), 15.

2. Mitchell Hammer, "The Intercultural Development Continuum (IDC)," Intercultural Development Inventory, 2019, accessed January 16, 2021, https://idiinventory.com/generalinformation /the-intercultural-development-continuum-idc/.

3. Milton J. Bennett, "Development Model of Intercultural Sensitivity," in *The International Encyclopedia of Intercultural Communication*, ed. Young Yun Kim (Hoboken, NJ: John Wiley & Sons, Inc., 2017), https://www.researchgate.net/publication/318430742_ Developmental_Model_of_Intercultural_Sensitivity.

4. "The Washington Post Names Evans Consulting a 2020 Top Washington-Area Workplace, Placing 9th on the List," Evans Consulting, June 16, 2020, https://www.evansconsulting.com /article/2020/06/the-washington-post-names-evans-consulting-a -2020-top-washington-area-workplace/.

Chapter 4

1. Chip Heath and Dan Heath, *Switch: How to Change Things When Change Is Hard* (New York: Random House, 2011), 17.

2. Heath and Heath, 28.

3. Katharine Schwab, "Readers Respond: Open Offices Are Terrible for Women," *Fast Company*, May 11, 2018, https://www.fastcompany .com/90171697/readers-respond-open-offices-are-terrible-for-women.

4. Claudia Goldin and Cecelia Rouse, "Orchestrating Impartiality: The Impact of Blind Auditions on Female Musicians," *American Economic Review* 90, no. 4 (2000): 715–41.

5. Eva Derous and Ann Marie Ryan, "When Your Résumé Is (Not) Turning You Down: Modelling Ethnic Bias in Résumé Screening," *Human Resource Management Journal* 39, no. 2 (2019): 119–30, https://doi.org/10.1111/1748-8583.12217.

6. Christina Gravert, "Why Triggering Emotions Won't Lead to Lasting Behavior Change," *Behavioral Scientist*, May 18, 2020, https://behavioralscientist.org/why-triggering-emotions-wont-lead -to-lasting-behavior-change/.

7. "The Promise and Perils of PlayPump," *The World*, July 7, 2010, https://www.pri.org/stories/2010-07-07/promise-and-perils -playpump.

8. Daniel Stellar, "The PlayPump: What Went Wrong?" State of the Planet, July 1, 2010, https://blogs.ei.columbia.edu/2010/07/01/the-playpump-what-went-wrong/.

9. Andrew Chambers, "Africa's Not-So-Magic Roundabout," *Guardian*, November 24, 2009, https://www.theguardian.com/commentisfree/2009/nov/24/africa-charity-water-pumps-roundabouts.

10. Nerdwriter, "How Dark Patterns Trick You Online," posted March 28, 2018, USA, YouTube video, 6:56, https://www.youtube.com/watch?v=kxkrdLl6e6M. To learn more, see https://www.darkpatterns.org/.

11. Peter Cappelli, "Your Approach to Hiring Is All Wrong," *Harvard Business Review*, May–June 2019, https://hbr.org/2019/05/your-approach-to-hiring-is-all-wrong.

12. Khari Johnson, "DeepMind Researchers Propose Rebuilding the AI Industry on a Base of Anticolonialism," *VentureBeat*, July 11, 2020, https://venturebeat.com/2020/07/11/deepmind-researchers-propose-rebuilding-the-ai-industry-on-a-base-of-anticolonialism/.

13. Khari Johnson, "AI Researchers Propose 'Bias Bounties' to Put Ethics Principles into Practice," *VentureBeat*, April 17, 2020, https://venturebeat.com/2020/04/17/ai-researchers-propose-bias-bounties-to-put-ethics-principles-into-practice/.

Chapter 5

1. Isabel Wilkerson, *Caste: The Origins of Our Discontents* (New York: Random House, 2020), 18.

2. Brakkton Booker, "White Woman Who Called Police on Black Bird-Watcher in Central Park Has Been Fired," NPR, May 26, 2020, https://www.npr.org/transcripts/862230724.

3. Center for Research on Environmental Decisions, "Get Your Audience's Attention," chap. 2 in *The Psychology of Climate Change Communication: A Guide for Scientists, Journalists, Educators, Political Aides, and the Interested Public* (New York:

Columbia University, 2009), http://guide.cred.columbia.edu/guide/sec2.html.

4. Lynn Davey, *Talking about Disparities: The Effect of Frame Choices on Support for Racial Equity Policies. A FrameWorks Institute Message Brief*, FrameWorks Institute, 2009, https://www.frameworksinstitute.org/wp-content/uploads/2020/03/disparitiesmessagebrief.pdf.

5. Davey, *Frameworks*.

6. Martin Luther King Jr., *Why We Can't Wait* (New York: New American Library, 1964), 65.

7. The Smart Chart blueprint has generously been made available at https://smartchart.org/.

8. Horizon Foundation, *The 2020 Vision for Health in Howard County* (Columbia, MD: Horizon Foundation, 2020), https://www.thehorizonfoundation.org/wp-content/uploads/2012/04/2020-Vision-for-Health-Horizon-Foundation-Report-FINAL2-pages.pdf.

9. Elie Wiesel, "Acceptance Speech," Nobel Prize, December 10, 1986, https://www.nobelprize.org/prizes/peace/1986/wiesel/acceptance-speech/.

Chapter 6

1. Christopher Bell, "Bring on the Female Superheroes!" filmed October 2015 at TEDxColoradoSprings, CO, TEA video, 15:40, https://www.ted.com/talks/christopher_bell_bring_on_the_female_superheroes?language=en.

2. Albert Bandura, Dorothea Ross, and Sheila A. Ross, "Transmission of Aggression through Imitation of Aggressive Models," *Journal of Abnormal and Social Psychology* 63, no. 3 (1961): 575–82.

3. Matthew S. McGlone and Barbara Breckinridge, "Why the Brain Doubts a Foreign Accent," *Scientific American*, September 21, 2010, https://www.scientificamerican.com/article/the-brain-doubts-accent/.

4. Samantha Schmidt, "'Star Wars' Actor Diego Luna Did Not Hide His Mexican Accent—and Latinos Heard It Loud," *Washington Post*, January 5, 2017, https://www.washingtonpost.com/news /morning-mix/wp/2017/01/05/actor-diego-luna-kept-his-mexican -accent-in-star-wars-sending-a-powerful-message-to-latinos/.

5. Caroline Heldman et al., "See Jane 2020," Geena Davis Institute on Gender in Media, 2020, https://seejane.org/research-informs -empowers/2020-film-historic-gender-parity-in-family-films/.

6. "If He Can See It, Will He Be It?" Geena Davis Institute on Gender in Media, June 23, 2020, https://seejane.org/research-informs -empowers/if-he-can-see-it-will-he-be-it/ (accessed December 31, 2020).

7. Maisha Z. Johnson, "What's Wrong with Cultural Appropriation? These 9 Answers Reveal Its Harm," Everyday Feminism, June 14, 2015, https://everydayfeminism.com/2015/06/cultural -appropriation-wrong/.

8. Robyne, "For Halloween, 'Molly of Denali' Creators Explain How to Dress Up like Molly," KTOO, October 25, 2019, https://www.ktoo .org/2019/10/25/for-halloween-molly-of-denali-creators-explain -how-to-dress-up-like-molly/.

9. "Why Web Accessibility Is Crucial for Digital Marketers," Bureau of Internet Accessibility, April 10, 2018, https://www.boia.org/blog /why-web-accessibility-is-crucial-for-digital-marketers.

10. "Facts about Americans with Disabilities," US Department of Justice, Civil Rights Division, December 20, 2006, https://www .ada.gov/busstat.htm.

11. Elise Roy, "When We Design for Disability, We All Benefit," filmed September 2015 at TEDxMidAtlantic, Washington, DC, TED video, 13:10, https://www.ted.com/talks/elise_roy_when_we_design_for_ disability_we_all_benefit.

12. Margaret Rhodes, "To Design a More Accessible Internet, Consider the 'Creative Layer' of Metadata," *Eye on Design*, August 3, 2020, https://eyeondesign.aiga.org/to-design-a-more -accessible-internet-consider-the-creative-layer-of-metadata/.

13. "Accessibility: Resources to Help Ensure Accessibility of Your Virtual Events for People with Disabilities," National Endowment for the Arts, May 1, 2020, https://www.arts.gov/accessibility /accessibility-resources/resources-to-help-ensure-accessibility-for -your-virtual-events-for-people-with-disabilities.

14. For more information, see https://www.rid.org.

15. Minal Bopaiah, "Time for Global Action on Mental Health," *Stanford Social Innovation Review*, March 30, 2016, https://ssir.org /articles/entry/time_for_global_action_on_mental_health.

16. Simon Kemp, "Digital 2020: Global Digital Overview," Hootsuite, 2020, https://hootsuite.com/resources/digital-2020.

17. Senongo Akpem, *Cross-Cultural Design* (New York: A Book Apart, 2020), 9.

18. Akpem, 9.

19. Adapted from Vu Le, "Content Creators, Here's an Equity Screen to Use as You Work on Your Next Blog Post, Book, Podcast, or Video," NonprofitAF, August 19, 2019, https://nonprofitaf .com/2019/08/content-creators-heres-an-equity-screen-to-use-as -you-work-on-your-next-blog-post-book-podcast-or-video/.

Conclusion

1. Sarah Spellings, "What Happens after the Wayfair Walkout," *The Cut*, June 27, 2019, https://www.thecut.com/2019/06/what-happened -at-the-wayfair-employee-walkout.html.

2. Edward Helmore, "Hachette Workers Stage Walkout to Protest Publication of Woody Allen Memoir," *Guardian*, March 5, 2020, https://www.theguardian.com/books/2020/mar/05 /hachette-woody-allen-memoir-protest-ronan-farrow.

3. Sheera Frenkel, Mike Isaac, Cecilia Kang, and Gabriel J. X. Dance, "Facebook Employees Stage Virtual Walkout to Protest Trump Posts," *New York Times*, June 1, 2020, https://www.nytimes.com /2020/06/01/technology/facebook-employee-protest-trump.html.

4. Rohini Anand, "The Connection between Diversity, Inclusion and Corporate Responsibility," *GreenBiz*, February 26, 2019, https://www.greenbiz.com/article/connection-between-diversity-inclusion-and-corporate-responsibility.
5. Katie Clarey, "As Employers Join the Fight for Racial Justice, Authenticity Is Key," *HR Dive*, August 17, 2020, https://www.hrdive.com/news/as-employers-join-the-fight-for-racial-justice-authenticity-is-key/583546/.
6. Communications Network, accessed March 7, 2021, https://comnetworkdei.org/.
7. "Reports," Communications Network, accessed March 7, 2021, https://comnetworkdei.org/reports.
8. Monica Anderson and Colleen McClain, "Americans See Pressure, Rather than Genuine Concern, as Big Factor in Company Statements about Racism," Pew Research Center, August 12, 2020, https://www.pewresearch.org/fact-tank/2020/08/12/americans-see-pressure-rather-than-genuine-concern-as-big-factor-in-company-statements-about-racism/.
9. "CEO Pledge," CEO Action for Diversity & Inclusion, June 2017, https://www.ceoaction.com/pledge/ceo-pledge/.
10. Rebecca Henderson, "The Business Case for Saving Democracy," *Harvard Business Review*, March 10, 2020, https://hbr.org/cover-story/2020/03/the-business-case-for-saving-democracy.
11. "Democracy Index 2019," Economist Intelligence Unit (accessed October 2, 2020).
12. Henderson, "Saving Democracy."
13. Henderson, "Saving Democracy."
14. Henderson, "Saving Democracy."
15. Edgar Villanueva, "We Can't Return to the Way Things Were Before. For Philanthropy, the Way Forward Is Reparations," *Inside Philanthropy*, August 3, 2020, https://www.insidephilanthropy.com/home/2020/8/3/we-cant-return-to-the-way-things-were-before-for-philanthropy-the-way-forward-is-reparations.

16. Kimberly Amadeo, "Why Military Spending Is More Than You Think It Is," *Balance*, September 3, 2020, https://www.thebalance.com/u-s-military-budget-components-challenges-growth-3306320; and "Budget," US Agency for International Development, updated March 4, 2020, https://www.usaid.gov/cj.

17. Villanueva, "We Can't Return."

18. Annalisa Merelli, "The Problem with the Gates Foundation's Award to Narendra Modi," *Quartz*, September 27, 2019, https://qz.com/1714568/why-is-the-gates-foundations-award-to-narendra-modi-controversial (accessed October 1, 2020).

19. Anand Giridharadas, *Winners Take All: The Elite Charade of Changing the World* (New York: Knopf Doubleday, 2018).

Glossary

accessibility: The design of products, devices, services, or environments so as to be usable by people of varying abilities or disabilities. Accessibility refuses to fault individuals for the ways in which they are different and instead emphasizes the rights of all people to be full and participating members of society.

anticolonial theory: A principal that calls for the continued examination of the effects of colonialism on societies, nations, and individuals and advocates for national independence, free from authoritarian rule.

cisgender: Denoting or relating to a person whose sense of personal identity and gender corresponds with their birth-assigned sex.

colonialism: The policy or practice of acquiring full or partial political control over another country, occupying it with settlers, and exploiting it economically.

dark pattern: See unethical pattern.

dehumanization: The process of making a person or group seem less than human and thereby not worthy of humane treatment.

DEI: A commonly used abbrevation for diversity, equity, and inclusion.

diversity: Differences—both visible and invisible—within a group of people. Differences can relate to gender, gender identity, ethnicity, race, Native or Indigenous origins, age, generation, sexual orientation, culture, religion, belief system, marital status, parental status, socioeconomic status, appearance, language and accent, disability, mental health, education, geography, nationality, work style, work experience, job role and function, thinking style, and personality type. Note that while a group can be diverse, an individual is not "diverse."

employee resource groups: Voluntary, employee-led groups of individuals who come together based on common interests, backgrounds, or demographic factors—such as gender, race, or sexual orientation—and whose aim is to foster a diverse, inclusive workplace aligned with the organization's goals.

equality: The state of being equal, especially in status, rights, and opportunities.

equity: A state of fairness and equal access to opportunity that recognizes that people have different needs.

framing: A way of presenting or structuring an idea that does not alter the attributes of the message but helps make the idea more understandable.

gaslighting: Manipulating people into questioning their reality, usually by denying the veracity of their experience.

IDEA: An abbreviation for inclusion, diversity, equity, and accessibility.

inclusion: An environment where individuals and groups feel psychologically safe, respected, engaged, motivated, and valued for who they are and for their contributions.

intersectionality: A term coined by scholar Kimberlé Crenshaw that describes the study of intersecting social identities (race, gender, class, etc.) and related systems of oppression. Intersectionality posits that identities and oppression are not mutually exclusive but rather intersect to create unique experiences.

model minority: A myth categorizing certain ethnic and racial groups (primarily Asian Americans) as hardworking, polite, and law-abiding and therefore worthy of economic success. It is often used to drive a racial wedge between Black people and other racial groups.

nudge/nudging: A way of presenting choices that encourages people to choose the option in their best interest while still preserving their ability to opt out.

perspective-gathering: Asking people about their experiences without projecting your experiences or beliefs onto them; operates in contrast to perspective-taking, which may feed stereotypes.

power broker: Typically, an industry insider who is familiar with other important individuals and groups and who has the ability to influence systems and groups.

predatory capitalism: Cultural acceptance of domination and exploitation as normal economic practices. Examples include corporate and financial fraud and unchallenged political corruption undermining trade unions, suppressing wages, promulgating economic slavery, and creating wealth by imposing debt on vulnerable entities.

privilege: Access to opportunities and resources that others don't have.

representation: Accurate and complex portrayals of people of diverse identities.

rugged individualism: The belief that individuals are independent and unaffected by the system, time, or context in which they live and that their success is the sole result of their hard work and no other factors.

tokenism: The practice of performing an inclusive act (such as hiring a person of color) only to prevent criticism and give the appearance that people are being treated fairly.

unethical pattern: An interface designed to trick users into doing things that benefit companies, not users.

virtue signaling: Publicly expressing opinions or sentiments intended to demonstrate one's good character or the moral correctness of one's position on a particular issue.

Acknowledgments

This book was written and edited on the traditional homeland of Nacotchtank, which was a site of trade for indigenous tribes long before it was called Silver Spring, Maryland. The people of Nacotchtank, or the Anacostans, spoke Algonquian and lived in proximity to the Anacostia River in what is now known as Washington, DC, and suburban Maryland. European infectious diseases and settler colonialism—which continues to this day—pushed the Anacostans out of their homelands and into what is now known as Ohio. I am in debt to the Indigenous people who are here today, living, working, and thriving. I encourage you to learn more about the native land you are on by visiting www.native-land.ca.

I have a great many people to thank for supporting me in the creation of this book.

First and foremost, my parents. There are no words to describe the depth of their unconditional love for a daughter who refused medical school, delayed marriage, denied them grandparenthood, and continues to challenge their every assumption. Somehow, they found a way to love a most difficult child, becoming my first models of equitable and inclusive leadership.

I must also thank my second parents, Johnnetta Betsch Cole and James Staton. Auntie J, you are all my life goals. Your generous heart is surpassed only by your incandescent mind. So much of this book is born from our conversations, and I hope to one day emulate you in how you have used your power and privilege to launch a thousand women's careers, including my own. And to Uncle JD, thank you for being the paragon of feminist husbands. You have shown Chris and me how extraordinary a democratic marriage can be.

To my in-loves, Carol Price, George Price, Elizabeth Price, Mauricio Correa dos Santos, Ryan Price dos Santos: thank you for your exceptional patience during all the holidays I missed, all the visits that got postponed, all the video calls I skipped out on while I was writing this book. Thank you for so graciously accepting me as a member of your family. And thank you for being the linchpin of my guerrilla marketing efforts for this book.

My extended family holds me up when the world conspires against equity and justice: Ravi Singh, Yogi Singh, Valerie Molnar; Kuju Uncle and Viju Aunty; the Bopiahs (with only one *a*): Balleappa and Tina Aunty, Cary, Anishya, Miel, and Zahn, Tilly, and Annika. A special thank-you to Veena Aunty, who has been my role model as a Kodava willing to speak out against the isms and phobias, including casteism, even when it cost her socially. Much love to the Prices, Paganas, and Steilings for putting up with me, celebrating my accomplishments, and loving me even when you didn't understand what the hell I was going on about. Thank you to the extended Nagel clan, including the Lorenzes, Bowies, and Michael Shera and John Hellyer, all of whom have made me seem much cooler than I am.

I am grateful for my many teachers over the years. Howard Ross and Leslie Traub for bringing me into the Cook Ross constellation. Tonya Hampton and Rosalyn Taylor O'Neal for sharing their brilliance and wisdom. Kimberly Dailey, my fellow four, who understands me like no other. Ladd Spiegel, who saved me from myself. At Bowdoin College: David Collings, who took me under his wing and read every book of South Asian fiction with me so I could do an independent study in my final year, showing me that there is no age cutoff for intellectual curiosity. Penny Martin for teaching me how to write with both my head and my heart. Paul Sarvis, Gwenyth Jones, and Gretchen Berg, from whom I learned my most important lessons about the creative process.

The people who make Brevity & Wit what it is: Shilpa Alimchandani, who keeps me honest and grounded; Jakob Wolf-Barnett, who went to bat for me when things were bleak; Sophie Greenbaum, without whom Brevity & Wit would not exist; Sabine Marx, whose multifaceted brilliance is our secret weapon; Arielle Etienne-Edmonson, who keeps me organized; Todd Zeldin, who turns ideas into reality with ease; Tarine Wright, who quietly delivers. *Thank you.*

Acacia Betancourt deserves a special shout-out for reading chapters in this book as I was writing them, and again when the manuscript was completed, and then providing invaluable design feedback for the cover. And a huge thank-you to Rajan Patel of Dent Education for allowing me to highlight his story and for his brave candor about his own lessons and growth.

The Berrett-Koehler family: thank you to Steve Piersanti for first believing in me as a writer and working with me to pivot the scope and focus of this book as my thinking evolved. Thank you to Shabnam McFarland-Banerjee for her general awesomeness, creating a space for JEDI writers, and being the truest of allies. Thank you to my sister BK authors, Radhika Dutt and Joy Wiggins, for giving me monthly doses of inspiration and community to keep me on the path when the going got tough. And thank you to the BK Authors group, the marketing team, and everyone at BK who earnestly tries to live up to the BK creed to make the world a better place through ideas.

Brevity & Wit is especially fortunate to work with many generous clients who demonstrate integrity and equity on a daily basis and have supported us through the years. I would be remiss to not mention by name Keith Woods and Sara Richards of NPR; Bob Etris and Jack Moore of Evans Consulting; Joe Shaffner of the International Center for Research on Women; Joyce McDonald, Melanie Coulson, and Gayle Ewer of Greater Public; and Jim Healy of Alluvus for their support, kindness, and patronage. And a thank-you to Kristen Grimm and Dennis Poplin of Spitfire Strategies and Sukari Pinnock-Fitts and Amber Mayes of Fifth Domain Coaching for generously sharing their intellectual property.

This book was written primarily during the COVID-19 pandemic, and I am grateful for the mind-saving Zoom calls with the ladies of 30 College Street, my fellow Bowdoin alumnae: Christina Stahlkopf, Jennifer Hoenig, Elizabeth Gordon, Marisa Zahler Raymond, Nanda Blazej Guajardo, and Janet Beagley.

Sharada Tilve deserves recognition as my own personal consigliere.

Dharshan Neravanda, his daughters Amaya and Sarani, and the Neravanda family all deserve my gratitude for a lifelong friendship that has kept the Bopaiahs afloat through thick and thin.

And finally, my twin true loves.

Few women are fortunate enough to marry a man who not only is *willing* to do all the housework and errands while she writes but who does so *joyfully*. You brought me back to life, Christopher Price, and taught me there is no love without affection for imperfection. This book would not exist if I had not met you. You are one in a million and well worth the wait.

And to my brother Mikhil, my alpha and omega: I owe you everything. Your tremendous mental discipline is my daily inspiration, and I dedicate the merit of this book to your happiness and joy.

Index

Page references followed by *f* indicate an illustrated figure; those followed by *p* indicate a photograph.

About the Author

 **Minal Bopaiah** is an author, speaker, and strategist committed to designing a more equitable world. With degrees in English, psychology, and organization development, and a lifelong passion for diversity and inclusion, Minal has spent her career cross-pollinating ideas in service of greater social justice for all.

After acquiring a bachelor of arts degree in English from Bowdoin College, Minal began her career in publishing and journalism, first as a production assistant in McGraw-Hill's Medical Publishing Group and then as the international and features editor of *Boston Metro*. She was the first press intern for Doctors Without Borders' New York office. And for three years, she served as the executive editor of *Subscription Insider,* an online business publication for digital marketers and information publishers.

She then used her knowledge of communications and marketing in the service of nongovernmental organizations dedicated to global development. In 2016, Minal was selected as a digital production fellow by Organizing for Action, the nonprofit advocacy group started by President Barack Obama. Eventually, she became the marketing and brand manager for Cook Ross, a diversity and inclusion consulting firm founded by DEI leader Howard Ross. There, she led a marketing team of two, creating a strategic plan that led to a 1,450 percent increase in website traffic, a 30 percent increase in inbound leads, a 120 percent increase in social media impressions, a 50 percent increase in event revenue, and 1,800 opt-ins to the company's email list in one year. During this time, she further developed her knowledge of the principles of diversity, equity, and inclusion, which she had primarily learned through her experience in graduate school and self-study. It was also at Cook Ross that Minal met her mentor, Johnnetta Betsch Cole.

Minal spent five years studying clinical psychology in New York. She was a student in Columbia's postbaccalaureate program, City University of New York's Master's degree program, and Fordham University's doctoral program. While fascinated by research on implicit bias, gender differences, and behavioral change, Minal decided to discontinue her doctoral studies after acquiring a master's degree (her thesis examined psychosocial differences in reactions to torture among Punjabi Sikhs and Tibetan Buddhists) because of the field's resistance to account for systemic sources of pathology. However, during this time, she was also working as an educational content specialist at Sesame Workshop—the nonprofit behind *Sesame Street* and its international coproductions—where she saw how social science research could be used to inform media programming and affect systemic inequality in countries around the world.

Minal's interest in system-level change led her to undergo a nine-month certification program at Georgetown University in organizational development and change leadership. It was in this program that she was first exposed to human-centered design. Given her background in psychology, she saw the wisdom of designing for how humans think and behave and began incorporating HCD into her work.

Minal founded Brevity & Wit in 2016 as a means of combining her experiences and interests in human-centered design, IDEA, psychology, organizational development, and strategic communications and marketing so that she could better help organizations achieve the change they wish to see in the world. Since its founding, Brevity & Wit has worked with numerous clients in the media, international nonprofit, and professional services spaces, including NPR, *Slate*, the International Center for Research on Women, Amnesty International, Johns Hopkins University's Center for Communication Programs, Evans Consulting, and Alluvus.

Minal's thought leadership has been published in the *Stanford Social Innovation Review* and *The Hill*, and she has been a guest on several podcasts and radio shows, including *The Kojo Nnamdi Show* on WAMU. She has been an invited speaker at many conferences, including the Forum for Workplace Inclusion and the Public Media Development and Marketing Conference.

Minal currently serves on advisory boards for Dent Education, a nonprofit that teaches design thinking, entrepreneurship, and making to Baltimore students, and for Bring Change to Mind, a San Francisco–based nonprofit founded by actor Glenn Close and her sister, Jessie Close, to end mental health stigma.

Minal lives in Silver Spring, Maryland, with her family.

www.brevityandwit.com
www.TheEquityBook.com

About Brevity & Wit

Brevity & Wit is a strategy and design firm dedicated to designing a more equitable world. We help organizations achieve the change they wish to see through an approach that combines human-centered design, behavior change science, and the principles of inclusion, diversity, equity, and accessibility (IDEA).

Brevity & Wit's services include full-service graphic design; web design and development; strategic communications and marketing; and IDEA solutions for teams and organizations, including keynote talks, experiential workshops, assessments, strategic plans, leadership development and coaching, and organizational design.

We pride ourselves in partnering with organizations to cocreate solutions that work for their unique challenges. We work with organizations from a variety of sectors and industries, with a particular focus on media, nonprofit, and professional services firms. Our clients include NPR, *Slate*, the International Center for Research on Women, Amnesty International, Johns Hopkins University's Center for Communication Programs, Evans Consulting, Alluvus and many other organizations committed to social impact.

To learn more about partnering with us to cocreate the change you wish to see in your organization and the wider world, visit us at www.brevityandwit.com.

Berrett–Koehler
Publishers

Berrett-Koehler is an independent publisher dedicated to an ambitious mission: *Connecting people and ideas to create a world that works for all.*

Our publications span many formats, including print, digital, audio, and video. We also offer online resources, training, and gatherings. And we will continue expanding our products and services to advance our mission.

We believe that the solutions to the world's problems will come from all of us, working at all levels: in our society, in our organizations, and in our own lives. Our publications and resources offer pathways to creating a more just, equitable, and sustainable society. They help people make their organizations more humane, democratic, diverse, and effective (and we don't think there's any contradiction there). And they guide people in creating positive change in their own lives and aligning their personal practices with their aspirations for a better world.

And we strive to practice what we preach through what we call "The BK Way." At the core of this approach is *stewardship,* a deep sense of responsibility to administer the company for the benefit of all of our stakeholder groups, including authors, customers, employees, investors, service providers, sales partners, and the communities and environment around us. Everything we do is built around stewardship and our other core values of *quality, partnership, inclusion,* and *sustainability.*

This is why Berrett-Koehler is the first book publishing company to be both a B Corporation (a rigorous certification) and a benefit corporation (a for-profit legal status), which together require us to adhere to the highest standards for corporate, social, and environmental performance. And it is why we have instituted many pioneering practices (which you can learn about at www.bkconnection.com), including the Berrett-Koehler Constitution, the Bill of Rights and Responsibilities for BK Authors, and our unique Author Days.

We are grateful to our readers, authors, and other friends who are supporting our mission. We ask you to share with us examples of how BK publications and resources are making a difference in your lives, organizations, and communities at www.bkconnection.com/impact.

Dear reader,

Thank you for picking up this book and welcome to the worldwide BK community! You're joining a special group of people who have come together to create positive change in their lives, organizations, and communities.

What's BK all about?

Our mission is to connect people and ideas to create a world that works for all.

Why? Our communities, organizations, and lives get bogged down by old paradigms of self-interest, exclusion, hierarchy, and privilege. But we believe that can change. That's why we seek the leading experts on these challenges—and share their actionable ideas with you.

A welcome gift

To help you get started, we'd like to offer you a **free copy** of one of our bestselling ebooks:

www.bkconnection.com/welcome

When you claim your **free ebook**, you'll also be subscribed to our blog.

Our freshest insights

Access the best new tools and ideas for leaders at all levels on our blog at ideas.bkconnection.com.

Sincerely,

Your friends at Berrett-Koehler